D0430615

The Legal
Context of Staffing

WITHDRAWN
UTSA Libraries

The Legal
Context of Staffing

Jean M. Phillips and Stanley M. Gully

Staffing Strategically Series

Society for Human Resource Management | Alexandria, Virginia | USA
www.shrm.org | © 2009

This publication is designed to provide accurate and authoritative information regarding the subject matter covered. It is sold with the understanding that neither the publisher nor the author is engaged in rendering legal or other professional service. If legal advice or other expert assistance is required, the services of a competent, licensed professional should be sought. The federal and state laws discussed in this book are subject to frequent revision and interpretation by amendments or judicial revisions that may significantly affect employer or employee rights and obligations. Readers are encouraged to seek legal counsel regarding specific policies and practices in their organizations.

This book is published by the Society for Human Resource Management (SHRM®). The interpretations, conclusions, and recommendations in this book are those of the authors and do not necessarily represent those of the publishers.

Copyright © 2009 Phillips, Gully, and Associates. All rights reserved.

This publication may not be reproduced, stored in a retrieval system, or transmitted in whole or in part, in any form or by any means, electronic, mechanical, photocopying, recording, or otherwise, without the prior written permission of the Society for Human Resource Management, 1800 Duke Street, Alexandria, VA 22314.

The Society for Human Resource Management (SHRM) is the world's largest association devoted to human resource management. Representing more than 250,000 members in over 140 countries, the Society serves the needs of HR professionals and advances the interests of the HR profession. Founded in 1948, SHRM has more than 575 affiliated chapters within the United States and subsidiary offices in China and India. Visit SHRM Online at www.shrm.org.

Phillips, Jean, 1969-
 The legal context of staffing / Jean M. Phillips, Stanley M. Gully.
    p. cm. — (Staffing strategically series)
 Includes bibliographical references and index.
 ISBN 978-1-58644-157-9
    1. Personnel management—United States. 2. Labor laws and legislation—United States. 3. Employee rights—United States. 4. Employee selection—Law and legislation—United States. I. Gully, Stanley Morris. II. Society for Human Resource Management (U.S.) III. Title.
 HF5549.P45957 2009
 344.7301--dc22
                    2009030884

10 9 8 7 6 5 4 3 2 1

Library
University of Texas
at San Antonio

09-0477

Staffing Strategically Series

ASSESSING EXTERNAL JOB CANDIDATES

ASSESSING INTERNAL JOB CANDIDATES

THE LEGAL CONTEXT OF STAFFING

STAFFING FORECASTING AND PLANNING

STAFFING TO SUPPORT BUSINESS STRATEGY

Contents

Introduction

In the United States, employment laws and regulations are numerous, and exist for several reasons.[1] Because employers decide on the structure of the employment relationship and the principles that will guide pay, promotions, and employee relations, they usually have more power in the employment relationship than do employees. Laws and regulations help to limit this power and prevent abuses. They also help to promote fairness and consistent treatment by prohibiting discrimination in employment and providing equal employment opportunity for everyone. Discrimination happens when employment decisions are not based on job-relevant knowledge, skills, abilities, and so on, but on factors such as age, sex, race, religion, ethnicity, or disability. Unlawful or discriminatory employment practices intentionally or unintentionally discriminate against people with characteristics protected by law.

Complying with staffing laws is obviously a good idea from a moral, ethical, and legal perspective, but doing so can also be strategic (see Table 1). In addition to avoiding the expense of lawsuits and the negative public relations that comes with litigation, legal compliance forces companies to hire and promote employees based on merit. Basing hiring and promotions on merit can enable better firm performance by enabling companies to hire quality people from all segments of the labor force. Because laws alone do not provide the tools to recognize and break down these barriers, proactively managing diversity is important. Successful firms often go beyond legal compliance in recruiting and retaining diverse employees.

This is not to say that staffing—in legal ways that support diversity—is easy. Not only are the numbers of women and minorities in many professions alarmingly low, a look into the talent pipeline is generally not a cause for optimism.[2] And even when executives support diversity and inclusion, middle managers and supervisors may not.[3] Understanding the legal context of staffing is an important foundation of effective and legal staffing, and is the focus of this book. However, it is important to note that making diversity and inclusion part of the organization's culture and values is also important to merit-based staffing practices that provide equal employment opportunity to everyone.

Table 1. Why Comply with Employment Laws?

Complying with employment laws:
- Enhances hiring quality.
- Enhances the company's reputation and image as an employer.
- Promotes fairness perceptions among job candidates.
- Reduces spillover effects (such as when people who feel they were discriminated against tell others about their bad experience with the firm and discourage them from applying for jobs there or doing business with the firm).
- Reinforces an ethical culture.
- Enhances organizational performance by ensuring that people are hired or not hired based on their qualifications, not biases.
- Promotes diversity, which can enhance an organization's ability to appeal to a broader customer base.

Because employment laws (and the courts' interpretations of them) identify what is expected and required of every employer, they clarify what is permissible. They also help employers hire strategically by promoting the hiring of the most qualified person, which enhances employee quality and thus organizational performance. Avoiding unfair discrimination thus helps companies better execute their strategies and reach their goals.

Given the traditional scope and depth of contemporary books about this topic, this book's coverage of the major government regulations and legal issues involving staffing cannot be done in great detail. *The Legal Context of Staffing* is not intended as a legal reference and *it does not constitute legal advice.* The purpose of this book is to provide an overview of some of the key laws and legal issues surrounding staffing, and to identify resources for additional information. This book will also give you a good understanding of how to prevent discriminatory or illegal staffing practices. Laws differ from state to state, and they evolve over time, so you should always consult legal counsel to ensure compliance with current local, state, and federal regulations.

First, we discuss various types of employment relationships, their legal implications, and the influence of labor unions. Next, we cover some of the primary laws and regulations regarding staffing, different enforcement agencies, and various types of staffing-related lawsuits. Finally, we discuss barriers to legal recruitment and hiring. After reading this book, you should have a good understanding of how to create a staffing system based on sound legal compliance grounds.

Types of
Employment Relationships

E mployers use different types of employment relationships to stra-tegically manage their workforce. Because different laws govern different employment relationships, we begin by discussing a variety of employment relationships and their legal implications.

Types of Employees

Employees. An employee is someone hired by another person or business for a wage or fixed payment in exchange for personal services, and who does not provide these services as part of an independent business. If a job offer extended by the employer is not accepted as presented, the employer and employee negotiate the terms and conditions of their re-lationship and create a mutually agreeable employment contract. Every employee has an employment contract.[4] If a written agreement does not exist, there is often an oral contract in place that in most instances would be just as enforceable as a formal written agreement. Even if a written or verbal explicit employment contract does not exist, there is an implicit employment contract reflecting a common understanding between em-ployer and employee.[5]

The employer must withhold employee payroll taxes (income taxes and Social Security taxes) and pay other taxes, including unemployment insurance and the employer's share of Medicare and Social Security. In addition, employers are covered by the many laws and regulations that govern the employment relationship, and they are liable for the acts of their employees during their time of employment.

At-will Employees. At-will employment is an employment relation-ship in which either party can terminate the employment relationship at any time for just cause, no cause, or even a cause that is morally wrong, with no liability as long as there is no contract for a definite term of employment. Although at-will employment allows an employee to quit for no reason, firms call upon it most often when they want to fire an employee for any legal reason or for no reason at all. In all states (except Montana), if a formal contract does not govern a company's employment relationships, these relationships are governed by the "employment-at-will" doctrine.

Although the courts generally have upheld the right to terminate at will, this does not mean that employers should casually terminate employees without giving a reason or without following normal policies and procedures. Companies should follow their formal discipline and termination procedures whenever possible to help avoid discrimination and wrongful termination claims. The at-will clause is best used as a legal defense to keep the organization from being forced to follow its own policies inflexibly.[6] For example, at-will employment allows an employer to immediately dismiss an employee who is behaving dangerously. Without an employment-at-will clause, a problem or dangerous employee may need to be retained throughout the company's process of warnings and suspensions. Case law establishing when or if firms can rely on the at-will nature of the relationship varies from state to state.

It is important to note that employment-at-will does not offer blanket protection to employers for all employee discharges. Exceptions to employment-at-will are created by existing contracts, including tenure systems, individual employment contracts, and union contracts. "Just cause" clauses in union contracts protect most unionized workers from arbitrary firings and limit the employer to only firing workers when they can show "just cause" that the person should lose his or her job. Federal laws, including equal employment legislation and the National Labor Relations Act, also protect against retaliation and discrimination.

State laws that reinforce and extend federal protections and state court exceptions (in particular, public policy, good faith and fair dealing, and tort law) can also limit employment-at-will. Most states recognize an implied employment contract as an exception to at-will employment. Implied employment contracts occur when an employer's personnel policies, handbooks, or other materials indicate that it will only fire an employee for good cause or that it will specify a procedural process for firing. If an employee is fired in violation of an implied employment contract, the employer may be found liable for breach of contract. A few states have also recognized a breach of an implied covenant of good faith and fair dealing as an exception to at-will employment. This covenant presumes that employers are generally obligated to deal fairly and in good faith with all of their employees. For example, firing an employee solely to deny an earned bonus that has not yet been received, or to prevent vesting in the firm's pension plan, is unlawful in some states. Every state recognizes retaliatory discharge as an exception, meaning that an employee may not be fired as punishment for engaging in a protected activity, such as filing a discrimination charge, opposing unlawful employer practices, or filing a valid workers' compensation claim, regardless of the employee's at-will status.

It is important for employers to make clear to employees the meaning of at-will employment, and what they can and cannot promise at-will job applicants or employees. The best way to ensure that an employment-at-will message has been adequately communicated to new hires is by publishing the policy on something job applicants and new hires sign. Signing an employment application, or acknowledging receipt of an employee handbook, produces a written record that an employee has read and understood the policy. Table 2 describes how to develop an at-will employment statement.

Contingent Workers. The Bureau of Labor Statistics defines contingent work as, "any job in which an individual does not have an explicit or implicit contract for long-term employment."[7] This describes anyone who has a job currently structured to be of limited duration. Contingent workers are outside of a company's core workforce. A company can engage a contingent worker in two ways: It can hire the worker directly or it can contract with another employer that has hired the worker. One of the primary benefits of contingent workers is that they can be quickly brought on board by placing a request with a temporary staffing firm or an employee-leasing firm. This allows a firm to adjust its staffing levels quickly without having to fire or lay off employees, which can raise unemployment insurance premiums and hurt morale.

There are several types of contingent workers, which are described below.

Table 2. Developing an At-Will Statement

Most courts will find an employment-at-will relationship if the at-will statement:

- Is clearly written in understandable language thoroughly explaining what the at-will relationship means.
- Clearly states that no company representative may change the at-will relationship through oral or written promises.
- Explains that the organization's policies and practices are not intended to create a contract.
- Is prominently displayed, such as in bold type, in a separate introductory policy, or set apart in other policies.
- Is repeated where appropriate in other policies and handbooks, particularly those outlining work rules and disciplinary procedures, and other documents, such as application forms and offer letters.
- Is signed by the employee, indicating that she or he has read and understood it.

"At-Will Employment in California," Bullivant, Houser, and Bailey, August 2006. Available online at: www.bullivant.com/showarticle.aspx?Show=4319. Accessed January 14, 2009; Trafimow, A.J., "What 'Employment At Will' Really Means to You," *Workforce Management* Online, January 2005. Available online at: www.workforce.com/archive/article/23/93/01.php?ht=. Accessed January 14, 2009; Personnel Policy Service, Inc. (2004). "Use At-Will to Defend Your Policies, Not as a Reason to Terminate." Available online at: www.ppspublishers.com/articles/gl/atwill_terminate.htm. Accessed January 14, 2009.

Temporary Workers. Temporary workers are a type of contingent worker who can be supplied by staffing agencies or directly hired by the company in which they work. Contract workers are a type of temporary worker who provide more specific, advanced, technical, and professional skills than do other temporary workers, and who tend to have assignments lasting several months to a year or more. Temporary and contract workers are paid by the hour, and are only paid for the hours they actually work. Temporary workers often do not receive the health and other benefits given to full-time employees, and, unlike employees, they do not raise a firm's unemployment insurance rates if they are dismissed. Because of the lower cost and nonpermanent nature of the relationship, it can be strategic to use temporary workers until it is clear that the additional talent will be needed for the long term.

When using a staffing agency, the agency can be considered the temporary worker's employer of record (rather than the company) if the company using the agency has the *right to control or direct only the result of the work* done by an independent contractor, and *not the means and methods of accomplishing the result.* This can shield a company using an agency from charges of age, race, or sex discrimination for the staffing agency's workers. The agency must also provide performance feedback and scheduling functions, or else both the company and the agency may be determined to be co-employers, both subject to the employment laws governing the employer-employee relationship.

It is important to note that firms cannot always legally exclude temporary workers from benefits such as health insurance. For example, employees of temporary agencies working at an unrelated company's place of business, unless specifically excluded from employee benefit plan coverage, are to be treated as the company's common-law employees for employee benefit plan purposes.[8] Employers therefore need to have a clearly written benefits policy that specifically excludes temporary workers, if that is their intention.

Part-time and Seasonal Workers. Part-time workers work less than a full workweek and can be contingent workers, but do not have to be. Some organizations have part-time employees. Seasonal employees are employees hired to work only during a particular part of the year. For example, when United Parcel Service hires more workers during the busy holiday season, and when growers hire laborers to harvest fruit, they are hiring seasonal workers.

Unionized Workers. In the United States, labor unions legally represent workers, organize employees, and negotiate the terms and conditions of union members' employment. In addition to wages and benefits, labor unions bargain over virtually all aspects of the staffing process, including working conditions, facility locations, staffing levels, job descriptions and classifications, promotion and transfer policies, layoff and termination policies, hiring pools, employment discrimination protections, grievance procedures, and seniority provisions. The terms and conditions of employment are contained in a contract called a collective bargaining agreement or a collective employment agreement. The inability of management and the union to reach an agreement may lead to either a labor strike or a management lockout.

Congress approved the National Labor Relations Act (NLRA) in 1935 to encourage a healthy relationship between private-sector workers and their employers. The NLRA was designed to curtail work stoppages, strikes, and general labor strife. It extends many rights to workers who wish to form, join or support unions, or labor organizations; who are already represented by unions; and who join as a group of two or more nonunionized employees seeking to modify their wages or working conditions. Employers also may not discriminate against pro-union applicants.

Companies that employ workers with a union operate on several different models:

- A closed shop exclusively employs people who are already union members. An example is a compulsory hiring hall, where the employer must recruit directly from the union. In 1947, the Taft-Hartley Labor Act declared the closed shop illegal. Although the NLRA permits construction employers to enter into pre-hire agreements to draw their workforces exclusively from a pool of employees dispatched by the union, construction employers are under no legal compulsion to enter into such agreements.
- A union shop employs both union and nonunion workers, but new employees must join the union or begin paying dues to the union within a specified time limit.
- An agency shop requires nonunion workers to pay a fee to the union for its services in negotiating their contract.
- An open shop does not discriminate based on union membership in employing or keeping workers. Some workers benefit from a union or the collective bargaining process despite not contributing to the union.

A collective bargaining agreement specifying that promotions will be based on seniority rather than merit influences the types of competencies the firm should hire. Seniority-based promotions make leadership competencies important hiring criteria even for lower-level positions because these lower-level hires are likely to become the company's future leaders. Even in nonunion companies, spillover effects from competitors' union agreements can occur as the nonunion companies adjust their pay, benefits, and terms and conditions of employment to successfully compete for new hires and prevent current employees from leaving to work for a competitor.

Although the influence of labor unions has declined significantly in some sectors of the U.S. economy, this is not the case abroad. In many countries, collective labor enjoys a strong presence. In some countries, collective representation differs radically from the United States in that collective agreements often legally extend to an entire industry sector, making even nonunion workers covered by the agreements and effectively "unionized." For example, in Brazil, all workers have to be in unions. Europe and Indonesia require employee representative bodies, called works councils, to offer workers a second level of representatives beyond unions.

Independent Contractors. An independent contractor performs services wherein the employer controls or directs only the *result* of the work. Anyone who performs services for a company is legally an employee *if the company controls what is done and how it is done.* Independent contractors must make their own Social Security contributions, pay various employment taxes, and report their income to state and federal tax authorities. From a legal perspective, whether a worker is an employee or an independent contractor with respect to the company determines the obligations the company has to the worker. If an employee is incorrectly classified as an independent contractor instead of an employee, the company can be liable for employment taxes for that worker, plus a penalty.[9]

The Internal Revenue Service (IRS) gives the example of Vera Elm, an electrician, who submits a job estimate to a housing complex for 400 hours of electrical work at $16.00 per hour. She is to receive $1,280 every two weeks for the next ten weeks, which is not an hourly payment. No matter how long it takes her to complete the work, Vera will receive $6,400. She also performs additional electrical installations for other companies under contracts that she obtained through advertisements. The IRS classifies Vera as an independent contractor.[10]

Classifying a worker as an employee or as an independent contractor can be tricky. FedEx Ground has long claimed that its drivers should be classified as independent contractors, who should not receive benefits and who are prevented from organizing under federal labor laws. Although its drivers have the ability to own multiple delivery routes and to hire employees to run routes for them, FedEx Ground also has numerous requirements governing their work, such as uniforms, attendance, and the display of company colors and logos on trucks.[11] FedEx Ground pays its contract drivers based on how many pickups and deliveries they make, but the drivers own their own trucks and must pay for their uniforms, supplies, gas, maintenance and other costs.[12] FedEx Ground contract drivers sued in California state court to recover expenses, overtime, and other costs.[13] In 2008, FedEx agreed to pay $26.8 million to settle the case.[14]

Companies can strategically use independent contractors to help control costs, temporarily increase capabilities, and bring in needed talents quickly. Independent contractors can thus be particularly useful for companies competing through innovation or low-cost strategies. Independent contractors often receive a higher salary than do regular employees, but do not receive benefits, which can make them cost-effective. Because independent contractors are often highly skilled, they may prefer to work on a project basis for many firms rather than be a single company's employee. Independent contractors also have greater control over the work they take on and the hours they work, which can enable people to work despite responsibilities preventing them from working traditional hours.

Outsourcing

An alternative to contingent work is outsourcing the work to another firm. This typically involves contracting with an outside firm that has a particular expertise to assume complete responsibility for a specific contracted service, not just to supply workers. Firms often use outsourcing for noncore functions such as payroll, landscaping, and food service.

Offshore outsourcing by opening a location in another country or outsourcing work to an existing offshore company has become increasingly popular for many organizations seeking productivity gains. In 2005, nearly two-thirds of all *Fortune* 500 companies used offshore outsourcing, some saving more than 70 percent in labor costs.[15] Offshore outsourcing can be successful if the work is relatively minor or intermittent, such as updating a software module or developing company web pages. Many offshore companies also possess international experience that can be useful. The risks involved with outsourcing are primarily the result of conducting work in two countries having different cultures, distinct intellectual property laws, and conflicting legal systems. A company must consider the nature of the other country's judicial system, local laws, and what would happen if the offshore company goes bankrupt. In addition, the company should ensure that an accepted dispute resolution procedure is in the outsourcing contract, including where the case would be filed if a conflict arises.[16]

Laws and Regulations

Social pressures often lead to legislation such as wage and hour laws, and equal employment opportunity legislation with which employers must comply. Common law, or court-made law, is the body of case-by-case decisions made by the courts that, over time, determines what is legal and what remedies are appropriate. Each state develops its own common law in response to federal and state legislation, and the nature of the specific cases brought before its courts. Over time, these decisions establish the permissibility of various practices as well as appropriate remedies for impermissible practices. For example, workplace tort cases, or civil wrongs in which an employer violates a duty owed to its customers or employees that leads to their suffering damages or harm, and employment-at-will cases are treated at the state level. Because case law differs across states, it is necessary to be familiar with the case laws in the states in which your organization is operating.

Although most employment discrimination lawsuits are brought under federal statutes, individual states' laws can be even more restrictive. A state's Attorney General's office can provide information about that state's fair employment practice laws.[17] State laws also provide extensive protection from employment discrimination. Some laws extend similar protection as provided by the federal acts to employers who are not covered by those statutes. Other statutes provide protection to groups not covered by the federal acts and protection for individuals who are performing civil or family duties outside of their normal employment.

Written laws passed by local, state, and federal legislative bodies create statutory law. These legislative bodies may also create agencies such as the Department of Labor (DOL) and the Equal Employment Opportunity Commission (EEOC) to interpret, administer, and enforce specific laws.

Constitutional law supersedes all other sources of laws and regulations, and particularly applies to the due process rights of public employees.

Laws Relevant to Staffing

There are several major federal laws that broadly apply to employers. Whether or not an employer is covered by a particular law depends on its number of employees and whether the company is a federal contractor. Table 3 summarizes some of the federal anti-discrimination laws that allow individuals to sue an employer for failure to hire. We will discuss each of these laws next.

Title VII of the Civil Rights Act. Title VII prohibits employment discrimination based on race, color, religion, sex, or national origin. Title VII prohibits not only intentional discrimination, but also practices that have the effect of discriminating against individuals because of their race, color, national origin, religion, or sex. Title VII explicitly states that race can never be used as a bona fide occupational qualification when making hiring decisions.

Under Title VII, it is an unlawful employment practice for an employer:[18]

1. "to fail or refuse to hire or to discharge any individual, or otherwise to discriminate against any individual with respect to his compensation, terms, conditions, or privileges of employment, because of such individual's race, color, religion, sex, or national origin"; or

2. "to limit, segregate, or classify his employees or applicants for employment in any way which would deprive or tend to deprive any individual of employment opportunities or otherwise adversely affect his status as an employee, because of such individual's race, color, religion, sex, or national origin."

Congress determined that intentional discrimination was established "when a complaining party demonstrates that race, color, religion, sex or national origin was a motivating factor for any employment practice, even though other factors also motivated the practice."[19] The Act, amended in 1991, is enforced by the EEOC and provides monetary damages in cases of intentional employment discrimination.

The largest employment discrimination lawsuit filed to date is a widely publicized discrimination lawsuit pending against Wal-Mart and Sam's Club. Thousands of female employees filed a class-action suit over alleged denial of advancement, denial of equal pay, and a denial of promotions and raises based on the fact that they were women.[20]

Clothing retailer Abercrombie & Fitch got into legal trouble for employment discrimination when it tried to hire salespeople who fit a particular profile. Investor Relations and Communications Director Lonnie Fogel once commented that the company is, "very particular about recruiting certain kinds of people to work as brand representatives in our store."[21] To the company, this meant limiting its recruiting to certain fraternities and sororities known for their attractive, predominantly white members.[22] One former Abercrombie manager said that a poster with images of the ideal Abercrombie white male and female hung in her office containing bullet points of the qualities an Abercrombie employee should possess. Desirable qualities for a male included being a fraternity member who likes sports, partying, and girls. A female should like to have fun, shop, and be a sorority member.[23]

In June 2003, a lawsuit was filed by the EEOC that alleged that Abercrombie & Fitch violated Title VII. Plaintiffs alleged that Abercrombie's recruiting and hiring practices that excluded minorities and women, as well as a restrictive marketing image, limited minority and female employment. The lawsuit began when several black, Hispanic, and Asian plaintiffs complained that when they applied for jobs they were steered away from sales positions and into low-visibility jobs such as stocking and cleaning.[24] Ultimately, about 20,000 people joined the class-action suit.[25]

Trying to create a particular "look" for a sales force is not inherently unlawful. However, the EEOC warned that, "If recruiters use a subjective or 'creative' component in the hiring process, the employer must carefully review the results for disparate impact. The company needs to consider whether this 'creative' component breeds discrimination."[26] Moreover, "Businesses cannot discriminate against individuals under the auspice of a marketing strategy or a particular 'look.' Race and sex discrimination in employment are unlawful."[27]

Table 3. The Key Federal Anti-Discrimination Laws

Law or Executive Order	Who Is Covered
Title VII of the Civil Rights Act of 1964 (Amended in 1991)	• Private employers with at least 15 employees • Labor unions, employment agencies, and educational institutions • Local, state, and federal governments
Executive Order 11246 of 1965 and Executive Order 11375 of 1967	Federal contractors with contracts exceeding $10,000
Pregnancy Discrimination Act of 1978	• Private employers with at least 15 employees • Labor unions, employment agencies, and educational institutions • Local, state, and federal governments
Americans with Disabilities Act of 1990 (Amended in 2008)	• Private employers with at least 15 employees • Local, state, and federal governments
Rehabilitation Act of 1973	Federal contractors with contracts exceeding $2,500 must engage in affirmative action
Age Discrimination in Employment Act of 1967	Private employers with at least 20 employees
Immigration Reform and Control Act of 1986	Employers with at least 4 employees must verify the employment eligibility of everyone hired
Worker Adjustment and Retraining Notification Act (WARN) of 1988	• Employers with at least 100 employees not including employees who have worked less than 6 months in the last 12 months and not including employees who work less than 20 hours per week • Private, public, quasi-public entities which operate in a commercial context • Regular local, federal, and state government entities that provide public services are not covered
The Uniformed Services Employment and Reemployment Rights Act (USERRA)	All members of the uniformed services (including non-career National Guard and Reserve members as well as active duty personnel)
Consumer Credit Reporting Reform Act of 1996	Employers who conduct credit checks for employment purposes (e.g., if an employee handles money, which may require being bonded)

General Provisions	Further Information
Prohibits discrimination on the basis of race, color, religion, sex (both women and men), or national origin	http://www.eeoc.gov/policy/vii.html
Prohibits discrimination and establishes affirmative action to promote diversity in race, color, religion, sex, or national origin	• http://www.dol.gov/esa/regs/statutes/ofccp/eo11246.htm • http://www.dol.gov/esa/regs/compliance/ofccp/fs11246.htm
• Pregnancy, childbirth, or related medical conditions • (Defines pregnancy as a temporary disability that requires accommodation)	http://www.eeoc.gov/facts/fs-preg.html
Qualified individual with or perceived as having a disability	http://www.usdoj.gov/crt/ada/
Individuals with a handicap	http://www.dol.gov/esa/regs/compliance/ofccp/sec503.htm
Protects people 40 years of age or older	http://www.eeoc.gov/policy/adea.html
Citizens, nationals of the U.S., and aliens authorized to work in the U.S. are eligible for employment	http://www.dol.gov/esa/regs/compliance/ofccp/ca_irca.htm
Must provide 60 days of advance notice of covered plant closings and covered mass layoffs of 50 or more people (excluding part-time workers)	http://www.doleta.gov/layoff/warn.cfm
Ensures that members of the uniformed services are entitled to return to their civilian employment after their service	http://www.dol.gov/elaws/userra.htm
• Employers must disclose in advance the company's intention to obtain a credit report and obtain written permission from the applicant or employee • The applicant or employee must receive a copy of the report and a written description of their rights under this Act before action is taken based on the report	http://www.ftc.gov/os/statutes/031224fcra.pdf

Executive Order 11246 and Executive Order 11375. Executive Orders 11246 and 11375 apply to employers with a federal contract exceeding $10,000, and prohibit employment discrimination based on race, color, religion, sex, or national origin. Among other things, these Executive Orders establish that any employer with a federal contract exceeding $10,000: "...will take affirmative action to ensure that applicants are employed, and that employees are treated during employment, without regard to their race, color, religion, sex or national origin. Such action shall include, but not be limited to the following: employment, upgrading, demotion, or transfer; recruitment or recruitment advertising; lay-off or termination; rates of pay or other forms of compensation; and selection for training, including apprenticeship. The contractor agrees to post in conspicuous places, available to employees and applicants for employment, notices to be provided by the contracting officer setting forth the provisions of this nondiscrimination clause."[28]

Affirmative action is required by the Executive Orders, which are enforced by the DOL.

Pregnancy Discrimination Act. The Pregnancy Discrimination Act prohibits private employers with at least 15 employees, labor unions, employment agencies, educational institutions, and local, state, and federal governments from discriminating on the basis of pregnancy, childbirth, or related medical conditions. Pregnancy, childbirth, and related medical conditions must be treated in the same way as other temporary illnesses or conditions.[29]

Americans with Disabilities Act (ADA). The ADA applies to private employers with at least 15 employees (including part-time and temporary employees) for at least 20 weeks during the current or preceding calendar year as well as to local, state, and federal governments. The ADA guarantees equal opportunity for individuals with disabilities or perceived as having disabilities and grants similar protections to those provided on the basis of race, color, sex, national origin, age, and religion. The EEOC enforces the ADA.

The passage of the ADA Amendments Act in 2008 broadened the percentage of the workforce entitled to accommodations. The new ADA instructs employers and the courts to use a much broader standard when determining whether an individual is to be considered disabled. Any and all mitigating measures such as hearing aids, mobility devices, and learned adaptations are to be ignored, with the exception of ordinary eyeglasses or contact lenses. The new ADA also provides a much more expansive list of "major life activities" that need to be adversely affected before a disability can be claimed, broadening the ADA's coverage to almost every employee.[30] Impairments that are episodic or in remission are considered disabling if they substantially limit a major life activity when active.[31]

Rehabilitation Act. The Rehabilitation Act requires federal contractors with contracts exceeding $2,500 to engage in affirmative action to promote the hiring of individuals with a disability. The Act protects qualified individuals from discrimination based on a disability. As with the ADA, qualified individuals with disabilities are defined as persons who, with reasonable accommodation, can perform the essential functions of the job for which they have applied or have been hired to perform. Reasonable accommodation means an employer is required to take reasonable steps to accommodate a disability unless it would cause the employer undue hardship.[32]

Age Discrimination in Employment Act (ADEA). Although some states, including New Jersey, prohibit discrimination based on any age, the ADEA prohibits employers with more than 20 employees from discriminating against any worker with respect to compensation or the terms, conditions, or privileges of employment because he or she is age 40 or over. Specifically, it is unlawful for an employer:[33]

1. "to fail or refuse to hire or to discharge any individual or otherwise discriminate against any individual with respect to his compensation, terms, conditions, or privileges of employment, because of such individual's age"; or
2. "to limit, segregate, or classify his employees in any way which would deprive or tend to deprive any individual of employment opportunities or otherwise adversely affect his status as an employee, because of such individual's age."

The Supreme Court has held that the ADEA does not apply to claims of "reverse discrimination" where "young" older workers (e.g., 50-year-olds) receive less favorable treatment than "older" older workers (e.g., 70-year-olds). As a result, employers may provide more favorable benefits (e.g., formal phased retirement programs) to older workers within the over-40 age group. However, employers may still not treat older workers less favorably than younger workers in employment.[34]

In New Jersey, state law protects all ages over 18. Older workers cannot receive more favorable benefits than younger workers. New Jersey law thus prohibits so-called "reverse" age discrimination against an employee because the organization perceives him or her to be too young.[35]

Immigration Reform and Control Act (IRCA). Under the IRCA, employers must use the I-9 verification form to verify the employability status of every new employee within three days of their being hired. This form requires documentation verifying a new hire's eligibility and identity, both of which must be verified. To avoid the appearance of discrimination on the basis of national origin, it is a good idea to make the job offer contingent on proof of employment eligibility.[36]

E-Verify is a free online system jointly operated by the Department of Homeland Security (DHS) and the Social Security Administration (SSA), which enables employers to determine the employment eligibility of new hires and the validity of their Social Security numbers. Other employers can enroll and use the system on a voluntary basis, although all federal contractors and subcontractors may soon be required to use the E-Verify system to confirm the employment eligibility of their employees.[37]

Worker Adjustment and Retraining Notification Act (WARN Act). In general, the WARN Act is a federal law requiring employers of 100 or more full-time workers who have worked at least 6 of the last 12 months and an average of 20 hours or more per week to give employees 60 days of advance notice of closing or major layoffs.[38] Hourly, salaried, managerial, and supervisory employees are entitled to notice under the WARN Act, although business partners are not. More details about what is covered are available on the Department of Labor's web site (www.dol.com).[39]

Uniformed Services Employment and Reemployment Rights Act (USERRA). USERRA prohibits employer discrimination against job applicants who may be called into military service or who volunteer for military service. It seeks to ensure that members of the uniformed services are entitled to return to their civilian employment upon completion of their service with the seniority, status, and rate of pay they would have obtained had they remained continuously employed by their civilian employer. The law also protects individuals from discrimination in hiring, promotion, and retention on the basis of present and future membership in the armed services. The Department of Labor enforces USERRA.

Consumer Credit Reporting Reform Act. Under the Consumer Credit Reporting Act, an employer must disclose in advance its intention to obtain an applicant's or employee's credit report and obtain written permission from the individual. The applicant or employee must receive a copy of the report and a written description of their rights under this Act before action is taken based on the report.

Bona Fide Occupational Qualification (BFOQ). There are situations in which a protected characteristic can be considered a bona fide occupational qualification or BFOQ, and legally be used in making employment decisions. A BFOQ means that the characteristic is essential to the successful performance of a relevant employment function. Only a qualification that affects an employee's ability to perform the job can be considered a BFOQ.[40] BFOQs do not apply to all jobs, and race and color can never be considered BFOQs. One example of how sex can be a BFOQ is in relation to employment in a setting that is exclusively used by members of one sex, such as a locker room.

It is important to develop a specific job description outlining the requirements and duties of the position, as well as a job specification detailing the corresponding qualifications of the individual needed for the position before beginning a recruitment effort. BFOQs must be based only on the actual inability of individuals with some protected characteristic (e.g., sex) to perform job duties, not on stereotyped characterizations.

Asking about protected characteristics that are not BFOQs during employment interviews is a mistake made by many uninformed hiring managers. Table 4 contains several inappropriate interview questions and an explanation of why they can violate various employment laws.

Table 4. Inappropriate Interview Questions

Court rulings and EEOC guidelines prohibit the use of all pre-employment inquiries that disproportionately screen out members of protected groups and are not valid predictors of successful job performance or which cannot be justified by "business necessity."* Although interview questions in and of themselves are not illegal, questions having an illegal impact should not be asked. Because the following five interview questions are likely to have a discriminatory effect on employment, they should be avoided:

1. *How many children do you have?*† Questions regarding marital status, childcare arrangements, and number of children may be seen as being based upon the applicant's sex. Title VII makes it illegal to deny a female applicant employment because she has or is planning to have children.
2. *What is your native language?* If an English language skill is not a job requirement but the employer requires English language proficiency, an adverse effect upon a minority group may result, violating Title VII. Inquiring how an applicant acquired the ability to read, write, or speak a foreign language is also inappropriate.
3. *What clubs or organizations do you belong to?* The courts may view this question as seeking information that is not job-related and that could result in discrimination based on gender, national origin, or religion in violation of Title VII.
4. *What is your height? What is your weight?* Minimum height and weight requirements have been found to be illegal under Title VII if they screen out a disproportionate number of minority group individuals or women and the employer cannot show that these standards are essential to the safe performance of a job in question.
5. *Are you able to work on Christmas Day?* Religious discrimination in violation of Title VII may result from asking a person's willingness to work any particular religious holiday.

* Griggs v. Duke Power Co., 401 U.S. 424 (1971).

† Based on Kucler, D.G., "Interview Questions: Legal or Illegal?," workforce.com, available online at: www.workforce.com/archive/feature/22/23/74/index.php. Accessed December 28, 2008; KFDS General Assistance Center, "Legal/Illegal Interview Questions," Office of Human Resources Management, University at Albany, available online at: hr.albany.edu/content/legalqtn.asp. Accessed December 28, 2008; "Legal Issues in Employment Interviewing," University of Kansas Medical Center, Equal Opportunity Office, available online at: www.kumc.edu/eoo/interview.html. Accessed December 28, 2008.

Equal Employment Opportunity, Affirmative Action, and Quotas

Equal employment opportunity, affirmative action, and the use of quotas in staffing are frequently misunderstood, and are often the subjects of debate.

Equal Employment Opportunity

Equal employment opportunity (EEO) means that employment practices are designed and used in a "facially neutral" manner. Facially neutral means that all employees and applicants are treated consistently regardless of protected characteristics such as sex and race. EEO requires an unbiased assessment and interpretation of applicants' job qualifications. The consistent administration of staffing practices is thought to create an equal opportunity for everyone (not just members of protected classes) to obtain a job or promotion. The following classes currently receive protection under EEO laws:[41]

- Age
- Disability
- Equal pay
- National origin
- Pregnancy
- Race
- Religion
- Retaliation
- Sex
- Sexual harassment

Affirmative Action

Affirmative action[42] is the proactive effort to eliminate discrimination and its effects, and to ensure nondiscriminatory results in employment practices in the future. Affirmative action began as a supplement to the Civil Rights Act's promise to end race discrimination in employment. Out of concern that ending formal discrimination would not eliminate racism in employment decisions, President Lyndon Johnson issued Executive Order 11246, requiring employers who received federal contracts to take extra steps to integrate their workforces. Through Executive Order 11246, federal contractors with contracts of at least $50,000—and with 50 or more employees—must have an affirmative action plan.

The goal of affirmative action is to provide employment opportunities to groups formerly underrepresented in employment. These groups, particularly blacks, Native Americans, Asian Americans, Hispanic Americans, and women, have been identified by the Department of Labor (DOL) as "protected classes." Affirmative action is also required for people with disabilities, disabled veterans, and Vietnam veterans. Although Executive Order 11246 requires that covered employers set goals for minorities and females, there are no laws or regulations requiring the setting of goals for the other protected classes (e.g., persons with disabilities and Vietnam veterans).

An organization may engage in affirmative action voluntarily, because a court orders it to, because it is a federal contractor, or because it agrees to as a remedy for discrimination that occurred in the past. Although it does require setting goals, affirmative action does not require any particular outcomes, including hiring a woman or minority for a specific job. In most cases, affirmative action plans identify voluntary goals and timetables for integrating workers from underrepresented groups into workplaces, giving employers a framework to use in developing recruitment, hiring, and promotion strategies.

Affirmative Action Plans. An affirmative action plan describes the actions to be taken, procedures to be followed, and standards to be adhered to in establishing an affirmative action program.[43] Affirmative action plans can include, but are not limited to, provisions for nondiscriminatory recruitment, training, and promotion. Procedures for internal recordkeeping, internal compliance auditing, and reporting are often included to ensure compliance and measure the program's success.

Although affirmative action only applies to organizations that receive federal contracts, affirmative action programs have brought or accompanied significant employment gains for women and minorities. In the first 25 years of affirmative action, black participation in the workforce increased 50 percent, and the percentage of blacks holding managerial positions jumped fivefold.[44] In 2008, however, only 22 of the *Fortune* 1000 CEOs were women.[45]

Affirmative action plans must apply to everyone, regardless of their age, gender, race, creed, physical ability, or national origin. The goal of affirmative action is to give everyone an equal opportunity to compete for employment and to participate in all employer-sponsored programs based on individual merit, which must be determined by criteria which are applied equally to everyone, and which do not systematically favor one group over another. Preferential treatment is only allowable in cases settled by courts in contexts of discrimination claims. A firm cannot legally decide to give preferential treatment on its own. Affirmative action plans should be temporary and be discontinued when the workforce is representative of the available population, and should be formally stated in writing.

Affirmative action programs may temporarily give preferential treatment to qualified applicants from underrepresented protected groups. Numerical goals are usually established based on the availability of qualified applicants in the job market or qualified candidates in the employer's workforce. These numerical goals do not create quotas for specific groups, nor are they designed to guarantee proportional representation or equal results. A contractor's failure to attain its goals is not in and of itself an affirmative action violation, but a failure to make good faith efforts to attain the goals is.[46] Rather than giving any protected group preferential treatment, it may be better for employers to identify the business-related characteristic they are seeking (e.g., someone with knowledge of and influence in the black community) and use it in making hiring decisions.

It is important to understand some of the key factors that determine the legal defensibility of an affirmative action plan, particularly if it requires giving preferential treatment to any subgroup. Several federal court decisions[47] have helped to clarify several factors that are important in determining whether an affirmative action plan that involves preferential treatment is in violation of Title VII; they are summarized in Table 5.[48]

Affirmative action extends to layoffs as well. One mid-1980s case challenged a school board's policy of protecting minority employees by laying off nonminority teachers first, even though they had seniority. The Supreme Court ruled against the school board, maintaining that the injury suffered by the nonminorities affected could not justify the benefits to minorities:

> "We have previously expressed concern over the burden that a preferential-layoffs scheme imposes on innocent parties. In cases involving valid hiring goals, the burden to be borne by innocent individuals is diffused to a considerable extent among society generally. Though hiring goals may burden some innocent individuals, they simply do not impose the same kind of injury that layoffs impose. Denial of a future employment opportunity is not as intrusive as loss of an existing job." [49]

Table 5. Affirmative Action Plans Involving Preferential Treatment

- *Affirmative action plans should be remedial in nature.* Employers found guilty of discrimination can be forced to implement an affirmative action plan to remedy the discrimination. Employers who have an imbalanced workforce but who have not been found guilty of discrimination may be able to justify an affirmative action plan to remedy the imbalance. Employers whose workforce is representative of the available workforce will have a difficult time justifying an affirmative action plan.
- *An affirmative action plan should not exclude all nonminorities.* Exactly how restrictive on any subgroup quotas can be is unclear, but an affirmative action plan that excludes all members of a nonminority group would likely be found to be illegal.
- *An affirmative action plan should be temporary.* Discontinue the plan after meeting the affirmative action goals.
- *An affirmative action plan should be formalized.* Actions taken under informal affirmative action plans (i.e., those lacking formal goals or a formal statement of the actions to be taken under the plan) have been found to be discriminatory.

Based on Breaugh, 1992; Kleiman, L.S. & Faley, R.H., "Voluntary Affirmative Action and Preferential Treatment: Legal and Research Implications," *Personnel Psychology*, 1988, 41 (3), 481-496; Rosenfeld, M., *Affirmative Action and Justice: A Philosophical and Constitutional Inquiry*, 1993, New Haven: Yale University Press

An equal opportunity/affirmative action statement should be included in all recruitment communications. Most organizations use phrases/acronyms such as "EOE/AA" (Equal Opportunity Employer/Affirmative Action), "Equal Opportunity Employer," or "An Equal Opportunity/Affirmative Action Institution." If these statements are ineffective in recruiting the quality and range of applicants desired, the employer may use a more explicit and proactive statement in recruitment communications: "Applicants from underrepresented groups are strongly encouraged to apply."

Quotas

Staffing quotas establish specific requirements that certain percentages of disadvantaged groups be hired. Staffing quotas are not legal except in very narrow circumstances. The goal of quotas is often to equalize the proportional representation of underrepresented groups in the company's workforce with their proportions in the organization's relevant labor market. The size and location of a firm's relevant labor market depends on the nature of the job. For example, for faculty positions, the relevant labor market is usually defined as national. For management and professional positions, the relevant labor market is generally defined as regional. For staff and laborer positions, the relevant labor market is usually defined as local.

By the late 1970s, flaws in affirmative action policy began to arise and reverse discrimination, or discrimination against white males, became an issue. In a landmark Supreme Court decision, numerical quotas were deemed illegal in college admissions programs.[50] The Court outlawed inflexible quota systems in affirmative action programs, which in this case had unfairly discriminated against a white applicant. In the same ruling, however, the Court upheld the legality of affirmative action per se. The case prohibited schools from considering race as a factor in admissions to promote racial diversity unless race is considered alongside other factors and on a case-by-case basis. In 2003, the Supreme Court ruled that undergraduate and graduate degree programs may use affirmative action in admission decisions if it treats race as one factor among many for the purpose of achieving a "diverse" class.[51] Affirmative action must not replace individualized review of an applicant, and is unconstitutional if it automatically increases an applicant's chances over others simply because of his or her race.[52] Although these are not Title VII cases, similar mechanisms are applied to them.

Employers are not required to have proportional representation in their workforce as long as they can show that they are not engaging in discrimination, but they are more open to lawsuits if they do not. Although affirmative action, preferential treatment, and quotas are not required by law, they are not prohibited either. Because numerical quota systems allow less qualified members of protected groups to be hired over more qualified candidates, there are limitations on their features and usage. A quota is most often used as a court-imposed remedy for past discrimination or as part of a voluntary affirmative action plan.

Enforcement Agencies

L egislative bodies at the local, state, and federal levels have the power to create, amend, and eliminate laws and regulations, including those pertaining to staffing and employment. These legislative bodies have also created agencies for the purposes of interpreting, administering, and enforcing these laws. The two federal agencies of the most importance to staffing issues are the Equal Employment Opportunity Commission (EEOC) and the Department of Labor's Office of Federal Contract Compliance Programs (OFCCP).

The EEOC

When the EEOC was established by Title VII, its primary responsibility was to receive and investigate charges of unlawful employment practices and, for those charges found to be of "reasonable cause," to try to resolve the disputes. In 1972, the Commission gained enforcement powers and the agency's roles and responsibilities have expanded with the enactment of new or amended legislation. Currently, the EEOC enforces the following federal statutes: Title VII, the ADEA (Age Discrimination in Employment Act), the ADA (Americans with Disabilities Act), the Rehabilitation Act, the Civil Rights Act, and the Equal Pay Act.

The EEOC receives between 75,000 and 80,000 charges each year,[53] and the agency pursues more than 400 full-fledged lawsuits annually.[54] Even companies with large, sophisticated staffing functions are vulnerable. In 2006, the EEOC filed a lawsuit against UPS on behalf of a Rastafarian who was told he had to shave his beard to be hired as a driver helper. It also filed a national class-action sex discrimination lawsuit against Lawry's Restaurants Inc. on behalf of male applicants who allege they were systematically rejected for jobs as food servers.[55]

The EEOC also filed a suit against Abercrombie & Fitch alleging that Abercrombie's recruiting and hiring practices that excluded minorities and women, and restrictive marketing image, limited minority and female employment.[56]

In addition to enforcement, the EEOC also encourages and facilitates voluntary compliance through tailored programs to meet the needs of employers, including small business and federal-sector employers; and through programs to educate the public on EEO laws. Another good reason to ensure that recruiters and hiring managers rely on objective standards and comply with antidiscrimination laws is that the EEOC is pursuing more systemic discrimination cases, which can generate awards that run into hundreds of millions of dollars.[57] All companies have to report and keep records as required by the EEOC, but federal contractors have special reporting and recording obligations.

The remedies available to the EEOC for employment discrimination, intentional or not, include:

- Back pay, or the pay awarded to a plaintiff up to the time the court rendered its judgment;
- Hiring, promotion, or reinstatement;
- Front pay, or pay a plaintiff is entitled to between the time the judgment is reached and the time the worker returns to the place of employment;
- Reasonable accommodation; and
- Other actions that will make an individual "whole" (i.e., in the condition he or she would have been if not for the discrimination).

When finding intentional discrimination, the EEOC may award compensatory damages for actual past and future monetary losses, and for mental anguish and inconvenience. It can award punitive damages as a deterrent or punishment if an employer acted with malice or reckless indifference, although punitive damages are not available against the federal, state or local governments. The employer may also be required to take corrective or preventive actions to cure the source of the identified discrimination and minimize the chance of its recurrence, as well as discontinue the discriminatory practices.[58] The EEOC has published a compliance manual to give organizations and employees guidance and compliance tools for employment discrimination issues.[59]

All employers with 15 or more employees are required to keep employment records. Based on federal contract activities and the number of employees, some large employers are also required to file an EEO-1 report annually.[60]

The OFCCP

The OFCCP is part of the Department of Labor.[61] It is responsible for administering and enforcing three equal employment opportunity programs that apply to federal contractors and subcontractors. The primary mission of the OFCCP is to ensure that federal contractors—with at least 50 employees and who receive $50,000 or more in grants, goods, and services—take affirmative action to promote equal employment opportunity and annually file appropriate affirmative action plans with the agency. The OFCCP's mission is to ensure nondiscrimination, to expand opportunities, and to make sure that all employment decisions are inclusive and supportive of diversity. The OFCCP primarily relies on compliance reviews and complaint investigations.[62] Although it does enforce affirmative action compliance, it focuses to a greater extent on class-action discrimination. The OFCCP conducts systemic reviews of employers' employment practices to search out discrimination. In 2006, the OFCCP conducted almost 4,000 compliance evaluations and recovered $51.5 million on behalf of workers subjected to unlawful discrimination. This was an increase of 14 percent from 2005, and 78 percent from 2001.[63]

The OFCCP undertakes compliance reviews for contractors flagged by a software program as having below average participation rates for minorities or women. The OFCCP also conducts reviews of contractors selected randomly and those identified through complaints. If it finds a violation of affirmative action or anti-discrimination requirements, the OFCCP attempts to reconcile with the contractor before referring the case for formal administrative enforcement. The OFCCP gives Exemplary Voluntary Efforts (EVE) and Opportunity 2000 awards to those companies who demonstrate significant achievement in equal opportunity and affirmative action. Although a contractor in violation of Executive Order 11246 may have its federal contracts terminated or suspended, such administrative actions are rare, and the contractor gets sufficient due process before this happens.[64]

How Does the OFCCP Define "Applicant"? Because they must track the gender, race, and ethnicity of applicants and analyze whether hiring practices, policies, or procedures have a "disparate impact" on minority and women applicants, the definition of "applicant" is particularly important to federal government contractors. Because affirmative action plans address the number of applicants from legally protected groups (e.g., age, race, gender, ethnicity, national origin), the definition of "job applicant" has important ramifications for many organizations. The OFCCP's record retention regulations under Executive Order 11246 require federal contractors to retain paper resumes and applications for two years if the contractor has at least 150 employees and a government contract of at least $150,000. Contractors with less than 150 employees or no contract of at least $150,000 must retain paper applications and resumes for one year. The OFCCP's regulations also require covered contractors to identify the gender, race, and ethnicity of each applicant, where possible.[65]

The legal definition of an applicant is particularly important with regard to two employment law issues:

1. Only "applicants" may establish a prima-facie (meaning "on its first appearance") case of unlawful discrimination regarding hiring decisions under state and federal discrimination statutes; and

2. Employers must determine who qualifies as an "applicant" in order to identify the gender and race of all applicants to evaluate whether its hiring practices have an adverse impact on men, women, or minorities.

The question of who is an applicant is critical to establishing the proportions of the applicant pool belonging to different legally protected groups (e.g., sex, race, national origin, etc.). Understanding the definition of an applicant can help employers minimize risk and protect themselves from costly audit defense.

To help federal contractors manage the burdens created by the Internet, which can generate thousands of applicants for a single position, the OFCCP published a final, revised definition of what constitutes an "Internet applicant" for federal contractors and subcontractors.[66] By "Internet and related electronic technologies" the OFCCP includes e-mail, resume databases, job banks, electronic scanning technology, applicant tracking systems, applicant service providers, and applicant screeners. This definition applies only to data collection and recordkeeping requirements under Executive Order 11246 (race, color, religion, national origin, and sex).[67] A person applying via the Internet (and related technologies) is an "applicant" if all four of the following criteria are satisfied:

1. The individual submits an expression of interest in employment through the Internet or related electronic data technologies;
2. The contractor considers the individual for employment in a particular position;
3. The individual's expression of interest indicates the individual possesses the basic qualifications for the position; and
4. The individual at no point in the contractor's selection process prior to receiving an offer of employment from the contractor, removes him or herself from further consideration or otherwise indicates that he or she is no longer interested in the position.

Consider a contractor who initially searches an Internet job database containing 30,000 resumes for two basic qualifications for a bilingual manufacturing supervisor job: a four-year business degree and fluency in English and Spanish. The initial screen for these two basic qualifications narrows the pool to 5,000. The contractor then adds a fourth, pre-established basic qualification of two years of management experience, which reduces the pool to 1,500. Finally, the contractor adds a fifth, pre-established basic qualification of experience in a manufacturing environment, which results in a pool of 85 job seekers. Under the rule, only the 85 job seekers meeting all five basic qualifications would be Internet applicants, assuming they met the other three prongs of the "Internet applicant" definition.

Contractors are allowed to use data-management techniques, such as random sampling or absolute numerical limits, to reduce the number of expressions that it considers, as long as the techniques are facially neutral and do not depend on an assessment of qualifications. For example, if the contractor receives a large number of expressions of interest, it can decide that it will only consider the first 200.

Contractors must retain records "identifying job seekers contacted regarding their interest in a particular position," and, with respect to internal resume databases, retain the following:

- A record of each resume added to the database,
- A record of the date each resume was added to the database,
- The position for which each search of the database was made, and
- For each search, the substantive search criteria used and the date of the search.

With respect to external resume databases, the contractor must maintain the following:

- A record of the position for which each search of the database was made,
- The substantive search criteria used,
- The date of the search, and
- The resumes of job seekers who met the basic qualifications for the particular position who are considered by the contractor, even if they do not qualify as Internet applicants.

Contractors must also keep all documents relating to tests and test results, interview notes, records identifying job seekers contacted regarding their interest in a particular position, and the race, gender, and ethnicity of each applicant or Internet applicant.[68] The OFCCP requires contractors to maintain only (1) those records relating to the analyses of the impact of employee selection procedures on Internet applicants, and (2) the impact of employment tests (without regard to whether the tests were administered to Internet applicants), because the OFCCP does not consider employment tests to be basic qualifications. Although the OFCCP will generally use labor-force statistics and census data to determine whether basic qualifications have an adverse impact on race, gender, or ethnicity, contractors should consider performing their own analyses.[69]

The OFCCP definition of Internet applicant applies only to people applying for jobs with federal contractors via the Internet and related technologies. For noncontractors, and for people applying for jobs through nonelectronic means, the Uniform Guidelines on Employee Selection Procedures[70] states that, "the term 'applicant' depends upon the user's recruitment and selection procedures. The concept of an applicant is that of a person who has indicated an interest in being considered for hiring, promotion, or other employment opportunities. This interest might be expressed by completing an application form, or might be expressed orally, depending on the employer's practice."[71] The EEOC, whose guidelines apply to all U.S. employers with 15 or more employees, is part of a four-agency group that issued a proposal similar to the new OFCCP rule in 2004. The EEOC could adopt that proposal as a formal rule, but as of 2006, the commission does not expect to take action on the proposal in the "near future,"[72] meaning that employers without federal contracts must still use the traditional definition of job applicant despite the burdens imposed by Internet applicants.

Thorough recordkeeping is also useful for purposes other than complying with legal requirements. Much of the information collected for legal purposes is also used in staffing system evaluation efforts; keeping it updated and available in centralized records is convenient as well as efficient. The information allows the organization to provide necessary documentation to justify selection decisions as well as defend those decisions against any legal challenges. For example, firms can use candidate assessment scores to evaluate recruiting source quality as well as to select applicants, and the same records may be used as evidence in a legal proceeding to show hiring decisions as job related and unbiased. Care must be taken to ensure that records on protected characteristics are not easily accessible during the selection process so that charges of discrimination cannot be made.

Grounds for Employment Lawsuits

Faulty recruiting, hiring, promotion, and termination procedures can all generate lawsuits. Employees who initiate lawsuits often reach all the way back to the hiring process to show systemic practices.[73] Below, we discuss several different types of staffing-related lawsuits and what is required for them to succeed in court.

Theory of Disparate Treatment

The theory of disparate treatment involves the intentional application or administration of employment practices, including recruitment, in a discriminatory manner. Disparate treatment is intentional discrimination based on a protected characteristic. If the employment decision (hiring or firing) would change if the applicant's race, religion, national origin, color, sex, disability, or age were different, disparate treatment has taken place. Disparate treatment can be *direct*, such as when it results from a company's policy to not hire older workers. It can also be *inferred* from situational factors or result from a combination of permissible and prohibited factors, both of which we discuss next.

Inferring Disparate Treatment. Disparate treatment can be inferred from situational factors. To establish this type of prima-facie case of discrimination under the theory of disparate treatment, the plaintiff must show:[74]

1. That he or she belongs to a group protected from discrimination (race, gender, etc.).
2. That he or she applied for the job and was qualified for the job for which the employer was seeking applicants.
3. That, despite being qualified, he or she was rejected. (The plaintiff does not need to prove that he or she was rejected

because of his or her protected status, only that despite his or her qualifications, he or she was rejected.)

4. That after being rejected, the position remained open and the employer continued to seek applicants whose qualifications were similar to those of the plaintiff.

Once these four aspects are established, the burden shifts to the employer to show that the discrimination is the result of a BFOQ that is reasonably necessary for the normal operation of the business, or the plaintiff wins the case. The employer must show that the discrimination is based on business necessity, or that it bears either a significant relationship to successful performance of the job or a significant relationship to a significant business objective of the employer. Demonstrable evidence of business necessity is required. The defendant may offer as evidence statistical reports, validation studies, expert testimony, prior successful experience, and other evidence.[75]

If the defendant is successful in establishing a BFOQ defense, the plaintiff then has the opportunity to present evidence showing that the employer's stated reason for the rejection was false and merely a pretext. To establish a prima-facie case, the plaintiff need not prove that discrimination was the motivating factor in the hiring or promotion decision; he or she need only raise an inference that such misconduct occurred.

A Mixed-Motive Case. A mixed-motive case of disparate treatment is one in which the employer is accused of having both a legitimate and an illegitimate reason for making the employment decision. Under the 1991 Civil Rights Act, a plaintiff may establish an unlawful employment practice by showing that a protected characteristic (such as race, sex, color, religion, or national origin) was a motivating factor in an employment decision, even if other legitimate factors (such as rule breaking or absences) also motivated the decision. A plaintiff only needs to prove that race and/or gender was *a motivating factor*—one of the reasons for the decision—no matter how small a role it played. If a plaintiff satisfies the burden of proof that discrimination was a motivating factor in the employer's adverse employment action, the employer is found liable. The burden of proof then shifts to the employer to cut off or reduce a plaintiff's monetary damages by proving to the jury that it would have made the same employment decision in the absence of the discriminatory motive. Under the mixed-motive analysis, the burden of proof is on the defendant to show that the decision would have been the same despite the plaintiff's race or sex. Under the disparate treatment method, the burden of proof is on the plaintiff to disprove the same thing.

The Supreme Court has ruled that plaintiffs do not need a "smoking gun" or direct evidence in showing a protected characteristic to be a motivating factor but instead can rely on "circumstantial evidence" that does not have to be linked directly to the employment decision.[76] This includes circumstances from which the jury can infer a discriminatory motive—for example, providing evidence that a black employee who had three unexcused absences was fired, but a white employee with the same number of unexcused absences was not.

Theory of Disparate (or Adverse) Impact

Disparate impact occurs when an action has a disproportionate effect on a protected group, regardless of intent or actual disparate treatment. Employment practices that are facially neutral in their treatment of different groups—but that have a significantly adverse effect on a protected group when compared with others—exhibit disparate impact and can be challenged as illegal discrimination. The only defense for disparate impact is when the disparate impact is justified by business necessity or job relatedness.

In the seminal disparate-impact case, the Supreme Court held that if an employer could not show a "business necessity" for requiring applicants to possess a high school diploma or pass off-the-shelf intelligence tests, due to the difference in pass rates for whites and minorities, the employer would be in violation of Title VII.[77] Examples of practices that may be subject to a disparate-impact challenge include written tests, educational requirements, height and weight requirements, strength requirements (e.g., being able to carry at least 50 pounds), and subjective procedures such as interviews. In larger organizations, the probability of disparate impact taking place somewhere in the company is greater because of the larger numbers of jobs and job families, or clusters of jobs in the same general occupation.

Assessment scores cannot be altered or changed to reduce the disparate impact on protected groups. According to the Civil Rights Act of 1991, it is an unlawful employment practice "to adjust the scores of, use different cutoff scores for, or otherwise alter the results of employment related tests on the basis of race, color, religion, sex, or national origin." This means that race norming, or comparing an applicant's scores only to members of his or her own racial subgroup and setting separate passing or cutoff scores for each subgroup, is unlawful.

Statistics. There are three types of statistics relevant for showing disparate impact: stock statistics, flow statistics, and concentration statistics. Stock statistics compare the percentage of men, women, or minorities employed in a job category with their availability in the relevant population of qualified people interested in the position. This is also called a utilization analysis. If the employment rate of men, women, or minorities is less than what would be expected based on their availability, they are said to be underutilized. Performing these analyses separately for women and minorities for each job group in the organization is the starting point for the development of affirmative action plans.

Employers must conduct stock statistics by job group (a group of related jobs) and do them separately for women and minorities. Although it is relatively easy to identify the number of people in each subgroup employed by the firm, it can be difficult to accurately identify each subgroup's availability in the relevant population. The percentage of women or minorities in the recruitment area who have the required skills—as well as the percentage of women or minorities among those promotable, transferable, and trainable within the organization—must be taken into account, but can be difficult to estimate or measure. Different utilization rates does not in itself demonstrate adverse impact; it only shows a prima-facie reason to further investigate an employer's staffing practices to see why the identified underutilization is occurring. Economists are often used in conducting utilization analyses, and technical, as well as legal, assistance is often advised.

Table 6 identifies a firm's utilization rates of women and minorities in the clerical job group relative to their availability in the relevant population. A takeaway from this data is that perhaps males may be underutilized in the clerical job category.

Table 6. Stock Statistics

	Job Category: Clerical Workers	
	Current Clerical Workers	Availability In Relevant Population
Females	80%	60%
Males	20%	40%

Flow statistics compare protected groups' selection rates, or the percentage of applicants hired from different subgroups, to determine if they are significantly different from each other. If a significant difference is found, adverse impact is demonstrated. This is the only one of the three adverse-impact statistics that can establish adverse impact by itself. The Uniform Guidelines on Employee Selection Procedures address the requirements for the computation and interpretation of flow statistics.[78] These guidelines state:

- Organizations must keep records that enable the calculation of relevant selection rates (also called applicant-flow statistics). Selection rates must be calculated:
  - » For each job category,
  - » For both internal and external selection decisions,
  - » For each step in the selection process, and
  - » By applicant race and sex.
- The 80-percent (or 4/5) rule determines compliance when comparing selection rates among subgroups for a job category. The 80-percent rule states that, "a selection rate for any race, sex or ethnic group which is less than four-fifths of the rate for the group with the highest rate will generally be regarded by federal enforcement agencies as evidence of adverse impact, while a greater than four-fifths rate will generally not be regarded by federal enforcement agencies as evidence of adverse impact."[79]
- The 80-percent rule is only a guideline, and provides for exceptions based on issues surrounding statistical and practical significance of the difference in selection rates (such as small sample sizes).

The courts have also found an adverse impact if the difference between the number of members of the protected class selected and the number that would be anticipated in a random selection system is more than two or three standard deviations.

The different selection rates (the percentage of applicants hired) of women and men for the Sales Associate job category is presented in Table 7. To apply the 4/5 (or 80-percent) rule to determine if disparate impact has occurred, we start by identifying the most favorable subgroup selection rate. In this example, we see that men were hired at the higher rate, and that 50 percent of male applicants were hired (100/200). Four-fifths of 50 percent is 40 percent. So if females were selected at a rate of less than 40 percent, then the subgroup selection rates differ enough to suggest that the selection method is discriminatory. We see that women were selected at a 25 percent rate, which is less than 40 percent, suggesting the possibility of sex discrimination in selecting sales associates.

Table 7. Flow Statistics

	Job Category: Sales Associates		
	# Applicants	# Hired	Selection Rate
Men	200	100	50%
Women	100	25	25%

The 80-percent rule highlights why targeted recruiting is important. If an organization were to simply target a particular subgroup for recruiting with little or no attention to talent, skills, and quality in the resulting subgroup's applicant pool, then it could unintentionally create a situation in which they would be likely to violate the rule. Simply increasing the number of applicants from the targeted subgroup without maintaining or improving quality can decrease the percentage of applicants hired from that subgroup, worsening the discrimination against that subgroup.

Concentration statistics compare the percentages of men, women, or minorities in various job categories to see if men, women, or minorities are concentrated in certain workforce categories. For example, half of an organization's employees may be female, but if women tend to comprise 90 percent of the clerical workforce and men tend to comprise 90 percent of the managerial workforce, then women may be underutilized in managerial positions and men may be underutilized in clerical positions. Concentration statistics do not establish disparate impact by themselves, but they can show a prima-facie reason to investigate an employer's staffing practices further to see why the differences are occurring.

In Table 8, blacks are concentrated in Sales positions (50 percent), Hispanics are concentrated in Clerical positions (65 percent), and whites are concentrated in Management positions (80 percent). This suggests that racial subgroups do tend to be concentrated in certain job categories and may suggest discrimination.

Table 8. Concentration Statistics

	Job Category		
	Sales	**Clerical**	**Management**
Whites	30%	15%	80%
Blacks	50%	20%	15%
Hispanics	20%	65%	5%

Establishing a Legal Case. The steps in establishing a disparate-impact case are:

1. The plaintiff must prove, generally through statistical comparisons, that the challenged practice or selection device has a substantial adverse impact on a protected group.[80] The defendant can then criticize the statistical analysis or offer different statistics.

2. If the plaintiff establishes disparate impact, the employer must prove that the challenged practice is "job-related for the position in question and consistent with business necessity."[81]

3. Even if the employer proves business necessity, the plaintiff may still prevail by showing that the employer has refused

to adopt an alternative employment practice that would satisfy the employer's legitimate interests without having a disparate impact on a protected class.[82]

Defending Failure-to-Hire Lawsuits

Lawsuits for failure to hire can be difficult to defend. In lawsuits over wrongful termination or failure to promote an employee, the employee's personnel record can help to establish that the decision to terminate or not promote was based on a legitimate nondiscriminatory reason. When sued for failure to hire, the employer has no history with the employee on which to rely. Providing an accurate job description to all recruits and using a standardized and well-documented recruitment and screening process is therefore very important for the employer, as this will be the foundation of the employer's defense if sued for failure to hire. Screening candidates using objective, job-relevant criteria with an established ability to predict job performance, and archiving all recruiter and interviewer notes, test and interview scores, etc., on each applicant can help defend the employer's employment decisions in court.[83]

One of the best ways for an organization to reduce the chances of being sued for failure to hire is to reduce the desire of an aggrieved individual to file a lawsuit. If an organization proactively and genuinely tries to generate applicants from diverse groups and subsequently treats all recruits fairly and with respect, rejected applicants may be less likely to engage in legal action. On the other hand, if an organization makes no effort to recruit from diverse groups and treats some applicants differently than others, or treats all applicants unfairly or with disrespect, applicants who are not hired may be more motivated to sue. Although important for all organizations, using proactive recruitment practices and attending to applicant reactions to the recruitment and hiring processes are even more important for larger organizations wishing to avoid lawsuits.

Fraudulent Recruitment

Fraudulent recruitment or fraudulent inducement involves misrepresenting the job or organization to a recruit. In a tight job market, or during periods of low unemployment among people with desired skills, employers may be tempted to exaggerate job benefits or make unrealistic promises to attract new hires. This runs the risk of a tort lawsuit based on a theory of fraudulent inducement to hire. A tort involves a claim that someone was harmed by a wrongful but not necessarily criminal act of another party, and does not require the existence of a contract. Damages must generally go beyond the loss of employment in order to make a claim. If an employer intentionally exaggerates what a job offers, it could be vulnerable to a charge of fraud. Although such claims of employment fraud are not common or easy to prove, they are becoming more frequent and are often won. In addition to sizeable jury awards ($10 million in the breach-of-contract case of a plaintiff claiming that an oil company never intended to keep its promises made while recruiting him), the damage to a company's reputation as an employer can compromise future recruiting efforts.[84]

In one fraudulent recruitment case, a state appellate court upheld a $250,000 jury award against a company for concealing information from a candidate during the recruitment process. The company presented a positive picture of itself and of the plaintiff's future with it and concealed its financial losses and the substantial risk that the plaintiff could soon be laid off. The court ruled that an organization may not have to divulge its financial condition to every applicant, but that full disclosure is required if statements are made to an applicant that would create a "false impression" about its outlook and the applicant's future employment prospects.[85]

Statements made to convince a job applicant to accept a position can be legally binding on the employer, even when no employment contracts are involved and even if the contract states that no promises about employment have been made. Making employment-at-will does not preclude a fraudulent recruitment claim.[86] Any negative changes in a recently hired employee's compensation or status, unless the employer can show intervening circumstances that arose after the hire justifying the action, may have the appearance of being taken in bad faith, potentially giving rise to a claim of fraudulent recruitment.

A variation on fraudulent hiring occurs when an employer uses fraud to keep an employee from leaving. For example, when a company bought a controlling interest in a machinery company, a man's employer assured him that "absolutely no changes would be made" that could hurt his job security. The man stayed, was soon subjected to a pay cut, and was eventually dismissed. The court allowed the man's claim for fraudulent misrepresentation to go to trial.[87]

To win a case involving an allegation of fraudulent recruitment and hiring, the plaintiff must prove five things:[88]

1. That the employer made a false representation of material fact;
2. With the knowledge or belief that it was false, or with an insufficient basis for asserting that it was true;
3. With the intent that the employee rely on it;
4. That the employee justifiably relied on it; and
5. That the employee suffered damages as a result, such as the cost involved in relocating, resigning from employment, or rejecting other offers.

Employers can reduce the likelihood of facing such lawsuits by instructing all individuals involved in recruiting and hiring not to make any statements about the company or the job that they know are not true, and not to make any promises concerning job functions, pay, benefits or job security that the employer does not intend to keep. Although it is only natural to want to present the job in a positive light, it is a good idea to qualify such statements so they are not seen as guarantees. Any written employment agreement should clearly spell out the terms of employment, including the temporary nature of employment if the job is not permanent, and state that the written agreement supersedes all prior agreements or understandings concerning employment. Written reminders that employment is at-will can also refute future employee claims of promises of long-term job security.[89]

Negligent Hiring

Negligent hiring is a relatively new tort theory based on the common law concept that an employer has a general obligation not to hire an applicant that they knew or should have known poses a risk of harm to third parties. Essentially, an organization is considered responsible for the damaging actions of its employees if it failed to exercise reasonable care in hiring the employee who caused the harm. These issues are particularly important when staffing positions that have or will have significant contact with the public, customers, patients, or children, or when hiring installers, maintenance workers, and delivery drivers, whose jobs would give them easy access to homes and apartments.

A company can be found legally liable for negligent hiring if it fails to uncover a job applicant's incompetence or unfitness by checking his or her references, criminal record, or general background. In order for a customer, employee, or other third party to win a negligent-hiring suit against an employer, the following must generally be shown:[90]

1. The existence of an employment relationship between the employer and the worker,
2. The employee's unfitness,
3. The employer's actual or constructive knowledge of the employee's unfitness (failure to investigate can lead to a finding of constructive knowledge),
4. The employee's act or omission causing the third party's injuries, and
5. The employer's negligence in hiring the employee as the most likely cause of the plaintiff's injuries.

An employer's obligation to its employees and third parties for negligent hiring depends upon whether that employer acted as a reasonable, prudent employer in hiring such employees. Pre-employment background checks are often the responsibility of recruiters. Because the law also requires organizations to respect applicants' privacy, candidates' backgrounds should be researched as thoroughly as possible without violating their privacy rights. Background checks should seek to identify felony convictions, but not prior arrests that didn't result in convictions, since these arrest records are generally protected by privacy laws. Contact all previous employers and keep a written record of all investigation efforts. Applicants should also be required to explain any gaps in their employment histories. If the organization can afford it, outsourcing background checks to qualified professionals can help to refute later claims that the organization failed to use reasonable efforts to learn about the employee's history.[91] Performing background checks routinely and consistently across all applicants helps to avoid possible claims of disparate treatment in how they are performed.

In some states, a company may have a duty to protect other employees from an employee whom it knows or should know is dangerous. Negligent retention is similar to negligent hiring, but it focuses on situations in which a company knowingly retains employees who have a high risk of injuring themselves or others.[92]

Negligent Referral

A growing number of states recognize the theory of negligent referral, which involves misrepresenting or failing to disclose complete and accurate information about a former employee. A former employer can be sued for negligent referral if the employee is involved in some incident at the new workplace that might have been predicted based on prior behavior.

Suppose an employee of Company A has poor performance or violent tendencies and Company A wants the employee to leave. Suppose the employee applies for a job with Company B, who calls Company A for a reference on the employee. Company A provides either minimal information about the employee or gives a positive reference, so Company B hires the employee who subsequently injures someone in his new position. Not only could Company B end up in court for negligent hiring, Company A could find itself defending a negligent-referral claim brought by Company B.[93] There have been several unfortunate incidents in the U.S. of nurses killing their patients and moving on to do the same thing at new hospitals because of hospital administrators' nondisclosure of information during reference checks out of fear of being sued for defamation.[94]

Reference checking is an important part of a thorough background check. Speaking with references helps to establish an applicant's credentials and potential fit with the organization and its positions. But many employers provide only dates of employment, salary, and title, fearing that revealing more information about former employees could expose them to defamation suits by disgruntled former employees unable to find new employment. To promote safe workplaces, more than 30 states have passed laws providing varying degrees of immunity to former employers who provide honest references about their former employees. It is too early to tell whether the immunity given to employers under these state laws is sufficient protection for them to feel comfortable giving truthful and accurate references about their former employees to prospective employers. Defamation, or "an unprivileged publication of false statements to third parties that tends to harm the reputation of the plaintiff in the community," is currently the most common cause of action used by former employees to challenge a reference given by a former employer. A growing trend is the practice of alleging defamation in wrongful-termination lawsuits, a practice virtually unheard of prior to the 1990s.[95] Recruiters can be trained in techniques to obtain needed information about candidates from other employers, but it can still be difficult to learn all that would be desired about a candidate from a reference check.

It is wise for managers to exercise caution in giving references for former employees, even in the states that currently have laws granting immunity to employers for giving references. Because very few court cases have interpreted these statutes, it is too early to tell whether these laws will provide adequate protection for employers. However, a blanket policy of providing only cursory referral information to avoid defamation claims may result in a company failing to disclose certain information about some former employees that could lead to equally expensive liability for the company on other grounds. Some experts believe that the best advice is to say as little as possible except in those situations where the employee's behaviors could endanger others in the new workplace. Saying nothing or providing a good reference for a bad employee could be riskier than simply telling the truth.[96]

Trade-Secret Litigation

Under the Uniform Trade Secrets Act, which has been adopted by most state legislatures, trade secrets can be any type of information, process, idea, or "know how" that is not generally known and gives the possessor an advantage in the marketplace. By that definition, trade secrets include a wide range of confidential business or proprietary information, such as chemical formulas, industrial processes, business strategies, and, under certain circumstances, customer lists. Almost all organizations have trade secrets to protect. In 2006, a sunroom manufacturer was ordered to pay $8.6 million for interfering with a competitor's former employee's noncompete contract and subsequently stealing a business plan.[97] To maintain business information as a trade secret, companies must take reasonable precautions, including requiring employees to sign confidentiality, noncompete, and nondisclosure agreements to prevent them from disclosing the information to competitors.

Trade-secret litigation can take place after an employee is hired by a competitor, or during the interview process. In 2000, Intel accused Broadcom of conducting job interviews of Intel employees to obtain confidential information. A judge determined that Broadcom had attempted to extract trade secrets during job interviews with Intel employees and granted a preliminary injunction against Broadcom. The court agreed and ordered Broadcom to change its interviewing and training processes so that new employees are neither encouraged nor permitted to disclose trade secrets of previous employers.[98] Even asking a candidate to list the customers with whom he or she regularly does business, or who the candidate could bring over as new customers, could lead to an accusation of wrongful conduct. Virtually any employee may be in possession of confidential information.

The best defense from trade-secret litigation may be the prevention of job candidate disclosure of protected information about other companies. Interviewers need to know what information is protected and how to question job candidates. Warn candidates at the beginning of an interview not to share a previous employer's proprietary information. When requesting a general description of the interviewee's job responsibilities and capabilities, ask the candidate to omit specifics of accomplishments that might include dangerous details. An example of a carefully worded interview question would be, "Without telling me anything about the actual recipe for a particular product, what is your role in developing new food products for the company?" It is also possible to ask the candidate, before the interview, to acknowledge, in writing, that he or she has been asked to avoid discussing confidential or trade-secret information.[99]

Sexual Harassment

Under Title VII, the ADA, and the ADEA harassment on the basis of race, color, religion, sex, national origin, disability, or age is illegal, as is retaliation against an individual for filing a charge of discrimination, participating in an investigation, or opposing discriminatory practices. Denying employment opportunities to a person because of marriage to, or association with, an individual of a particular race, religion, national origin, or an individual with a disability is also illegal.[100]

Title VII's broad prohibitions against sex discrimination specifically cover sexual harassment, which includes practices ranging from direct requests for sexual favors to workplace conditions that create a hostile environment for persons of either gender, including same-sex harassment. The "hostile environment" standard also applies to harassment on the bases of race, color, national origin, religion, age, and disability. Sexual harassment is recognized as intentional discrimination and thus companies may be subject to punitive and compensatory damages by a jury.

EEOC Best Practices

In addition to enforcing EEO laws, the EEOC provides programs to educate the public and employers on EEO laws and EEO compliance. One of the ways it does this is by identifying specific examples of good EEO and diversity programs and deriving examples of "best practices" that other companies might successfully emulate. The EEOC defines a best staffing practice as one that:[101]

- Complies with the law,
- Promotes equal employment opportunity,
- Addresses one or more barriers that adversely affect equal employment opportunity,
- Manifests management commitment and accountability,
- Ensures management and employee communication,
- Produces noteworthy results, and
- Does not cause or result in unfairness.

To help employers comply with anti-discrimination laws, the EEOC has identified a set of best practices employers can use to promote equal employment opportunity and address barriers to equal employment opportunity.[102] The importance of top management commitment in executing these practices and making them work cannot be overemphasized. This general set of key elements that support successful EEO programs corresponds to the acronym SPLENDID:[103]

- **S**tudy—know the laws and standards, remove EEO barriers, and seek assistance from the EEOC, professional consultants, associations, or groups, etc.
- **P**lan—know the relevant workforce and demographics, define the problem(s), propose solutions, and develop strategies for achieving them.
- **L**ead—have all levels of management champion the cause and provide

leadership for EEO implementation at all organizational levels.

- **E**ncourage—link pay and performance for how employees interact, support, and respect each other.
- **N**otice—monitor the impact of EEO practices; ensure that unfairness does not occur as a result of a corrective strategy.
- **D**iscussion—communicate and reinforce the message that diversity is a business asset.
- **I**nclusion—bring all employees and groups into the analysis, planning, and implementation process.
- **D**edication—assign needed resources and stay persistent; investment in EEO may take a little while to pay off.

Barriers to Legally Defensible Staffing

Strategically responding to the legal context surrounding staffing requires leveraging laws and guidelines to employ and retain the employees who will best help the firm compete and execute its business strategy. In addition to obeying staffing laws, it is critical that organizations identify and reduce the barriers that exist to legally defensible staffing and to providing equal employment opportunity.

Many barriers to EEO exist. Some of these barriers tend to be specific to a particular employer, rather than being societal or cultural in nature. Other general barriers based in societal or cultural practices or norms tend to be external to the employer. Next, we describe some of the general and specific barriers to EEO.

General Barriers

A report of the EEOC identified barriers to EEO that tend to exist across most hiring situations.[104] These barriers are rooted in decision-making and psychological factors, as well as unawareness. Because understanding and proactively addressing these barriers can minimize their impact and reduce the chances that an organization is discriminating unintentionally or intentionally in its staffing practices, we discuss each next.

The "Like Me" Bias. People tend to associate with other people who they perceive to be like themselves. This bias is part of human nature, and may be conscious or unconscious. Although it can create a higher comfort level in working relationships, the "like me" bias can also lead to a tendency to employ and work with people like oneself in terms of protected characteristics such as race, color, sex, disability, and age, and an unwillingness to employ people unlike oneself. Perceived cultural and religious differences and ethnocentrism can feed on the "like me" bias and may result in the restriction of EEO.

Because the "like me" bias can influence the assessment of performance norms, there may be a perception that someone "different" is less able to do the job and that someone "like me" is more able to do the job. For example, a male scientist who tends to believe that women make poor scientists is unlikely to hire a female scientist. This perception can influence targeted recruitment efforts and further reduce equal employment opportunities for minorities, women, persons with disabilities, and older workers.

Stereotypes. A stereotype is a belief about an individual or a group based on the idea that everyone in a particular group will behave the same way. "All men are strong," "all women are sensitive," and "people who look a certain way are dangerous" are all examples of stereotypes. Stereotypes are harmful because they judge an individual based solely on his or her being part of a particular group, regardless of his or her unique identity.

People may have stereotypes of other individuals based on their race, color, religion, national origin, sex, disability, or age. Stereotypes are often negative and erroneous, and thus adversely affect the targeted individuals.[105] Because stereotypes can breed subtle racism, sexism, prejudice, and discomfort, they must be addressed in the EEO context. Recruiters and hiring managers may have stereotypes of what makes a good employee that, if they are the underlying beliefs and attitudes that form the bases of targeted recruiting decisions, can adversely affect equal employment opportunities.

A common example of stereotyping occurs when rejecting an applicant as "overqualified." An employer may assume that a highly experienced person will have no interest in a lower position, or will soon leave for something better. Although this assumption may be true, case law says that a person who is overqualified is, by definition, qualified, so the person cannot be rejected on that basis. Also, if a person is truly qualified but not hired, the candidate may assume that age discrimination occurred. The best solution is to ask the candidate why he or she is interested in the position—they may honestly be looking to change careers or seeking a job with less responsibility. If there is evidence that the individual has done a lot of job-hopping, we are no longer simply speculating about whether they will stay in the job and have a more solid basis for rejecting them.[106]

Ignorance. Some employers, particularly smaller organizations, are not aware of all of the requirements of equal employment opportunity and may discriminate out of ignorance. Although it is not an effective legal defense, organizations may not know how the law applies to them because they have received poor or inaccurate advice. Even the largest employers may have individual hiring managers and recruiters who are not well versed in employment laws. As noted by the EEOC, to a large degree, stereotyping feeds on ignorance, but the repercussions of ignorance go much farther than stereotyping.[107]

Prejudice. It is also possible that outright bigotry still occurs on the part of an employer or its management for or against a targeted group, despite Title VII now having been in existence for more than 40 years.[108] Even if an organization has a strong commitment to equal employment opportunity, it is possible that the beliefs and actions of individual hiring managers or recruiters are inconsistent with the organization's policies and values. Organizations can help to reduce the occurrence of prejudice in recruitment and selection by carefully selecting and training hiring managers and recruiters, evaluating their performance, and tracking the diversity of the candidates recruited and hired by different recruiters and hiring managers to identify possible discriminatory trends that warrant further investigation and attention.

Perception of Loss by Persons Threatened by EEO Practices. As voluntary efforts are made by companies to address EEO and fairness concerns, individuals of groups who traditionally have been the predominant employees of a particular workforce or occupation may grow anxious or angry. They may view themselves as losing employment opportunities. If they perceive a direct threat to their own equal employment opportunities, they may feel that they need to protect their own prospects by impeding the prospects of others.[109] This can influence employees' willingness to refer diverse candidates for a position, objectively screen diverse recruits, and help to persuade diverse recruits that they are good fits with the organization and that they should accept extended job offers.

Hiring Managers. Hiring managers often lack an understanding of employment law and may be unaware that the same anti-discrimination laws that apply to employees apply equally to applicants. Hiring managers are often untrained and unprepared to ask the right kinds of questions during an interview. The most common problematic line of inquiry claims stems from questions related to childcare and child rearing. If a hiring manager is concerned that someone may not be able to come to work because of childcare issues, instead of asking about the candidate's childcare arrangements, the manager should ask the candidate directly how often he or she misses work. Asking questions related to attendance and productivity are entirely appropriate.[110]

Training hiring managers in employment discrimination and bias laws is critical. In one successful discrimination case, a federal court of appeals found that a car dealership's hiring managers had never been trained concerning bias laws. The court wrote, "Leaving managers with hiring authority in ignorance of the basic features of the discrimination laws is an 'extraordinary mistake' for a company to make."[111]

Specific Barriers

Unlike the general barriers just discussed, there are additional barriers to equal employment opportunity that tend to be specific to an employer. There are too many possible specific barriers to equal employment opportunity to provide an exhaustive list, but in Table 9 we summarize some of the more common, specific barriers identified by the EEOC.[112]

Table 9. Barriers to Equal Employment Opportunity Identified by the EEOC[*]

Barriers to Recruiting:

- Failing to advertise widely;
- Recruitment practices that overlook or fail to seek all qualified individuals;
- Reliance on informal networks of recruitment or word-of-mouth; and
- Having no formal systems for recruitment.

Barriers to Advancement and Promotion:

- Deficient feedback, performance evaluation, and promotion processes;
- Little or no access to informal networks of communication;
- Different standards of performance, disparate treatment;
- Lack of equal access to assignments that provide key career experiences, visibility, and interaction with senior managers; and
- EEO directors not included in recruitment process for higher levels.

Barriers in Terms and Conditions:

- Unequal pay;
- Counterproductive behavior and harassment in the workplace;
- Employer policies that are not family friendly;
- Inflexible hours and working conditions; and
- Failing to provide reasonable accommodation to qualified individuals with disabilities.

Barriers in Termination and Downsizing:

- Unfairness of standards used in making decisions, differences in benefits given;
- Inadequate planning;
- Lack of adequate incentives to encourage voluntary separations;
- Lack of communication between employers and employees; and
- Failure to provide counseling, job placement assistance, and training.

[*]The U.S. Equal Employment Opportunity Commission, 1997.

Summary

Given the many federal and state regulations affecting staffing practices, it is clear that those involved in staffing activities need to thoroughly understand them. Failure to comply with government regulations, even if unintentional, can have adverse consequences. Fortunately, the government has tried to help organizations to comply with the regulations by providing best practices and encouraging organizations to be proactive in resolving any underrepresentation that might exist in their workforces. In addition to avoiding legal trouble, many organizations also realize the benefits of an expanded candidate pool and better quality hires when legal compliance leads to greater recruitment and selection of previously overlooked sources of talent.

Endnotes

1. See Phillips, J.M. & Gully, S.M. *Strategic Staffing*, 2009. Upper Saddle River, NJ: Prentice Hall.
2. Diversity Officer Magazine (2009). Mentoring a Diverse Workforce. Diversityofficermagazine.com. Available online at: diversityofficermagazine.com/magazine/?page_id=285. Accessed July 16, 2009.
3. Novations (2009). *The Changing Face of Diversity and Inclusion: Then, Now, and Tomorrow.* Boston, MA: Novations.
4. Moscardelli, A.M. (2004). "The Essentials of an Employment Contract." LawNow, December. Available online at: findarticles.com/p/articles/mi_m0OJX/is_3_29/ai_n25100577/. Accessed July 16, 2009.
5. See Mende, B., "Controlling Risk With Employment Contracts," CareerJournal.com, January 26, 1998, available online at: www.careerjournal.com/myc/negotiate/19980126-mende.html. Accessed December 1, 2006.
6. Personnel Policy Service, Inc. (2004). "Use At-Will to Defend Your Policies, Not as a Reason to Terminate." Available online at: www.ppspublishers.com/articles/gl/atwill_terminate.htm. Accessed December 23, 2008.
7. See Polivka, A.E. & Nardone, T., "On the Definition of 'Contingent Work,' " Monthly Labor Review, December 1989, pp. 9-16.
8. *Burrey v. Pacific Gas & Electric*, et al., 159 F.3d 388, 98 D.A.R. 10924 (9th Cir. 1998).
9. Internal Revenue Service, "Independent Contractors Versus Employees," www.irs.gov/businesses/small/article/0,,id=99921,00.html.
10. Ibid.
11. Frauenheim, E., "FedEx Suffers Independent Contractor Setback," *Workforce Management* Online, December 26, 2007. Available online at: www.workforce.com/section/00/article/25/28/35.html. Accessed January 14, 2009.
12. Foust, D., "The Ground War at FedEx," *BusinessWeek*, November 28, 2005. Available online at: www.businessweek.com/magazine/content/05_48/b3961086.htm. Accessed January 14, 2009.
13. Speizer, I., "FedEx Court Decision Is a Wake-Up Call," *Workforce Management* Online, December 2004. Available online at: www.workforce.com/archive/feature/23/90/25/239030.php. Accessed January 14, 2009.
14. "FedEx Settles Suit Over Contract Drivers," *Los Angeles Times*, December 6, 2008. Available online at:www.latimes.com/business/la-fi-fedex6-2008dec06,0,4149288.story. Accessed January 14, 2009.
15. Petershack, R., "Consider the Legal Issues Before Outsourcing Offshore," Wisconsin Technology Network, July 18, 2005, available online at: wistechnology.com/article.php?id=2007. Accessed December 23, 2008.
16. Ibid.
17. See also www.hrtools.com/hressentials/p05_0160.asp for a description of employment laws in different states.

[18] See SEC. 2000e-2. [Section 703] of the Civil Rights Act of 1964, available online at: www.eeoc.gov/policy/vii.html.

[19] Sec. 703 (m) of Title VII.

[20] Glater, J.D., "Attention Wal-Mart Plaintiffs: Hurdles Ahead," *The New York Times*, June 27, 2004, available online at: select.nytimes.com/gst/abstract.html?res=F00 B13FD3D5C0C748EDDAF0894DC404482&n=Top%2fNews%2fBusiness%2fC ompanies%2fWal%2dMart%20Stores%20Inc%2e. Accessed December 23, 2008.

[21] Marino-Nachison, D., "TMF Interview With Abercrombie & Fitch Investor Relations and Communications Director Lonnie Fogel," The Motley Fool, June 7, 1999, available online at: www.fool.com/foolaudio/transcripts/1999/stocktalk990607_abercrombie.htm. Accessed December 23, 2008.

[22] Gerstein, J., "Suit Charged Company Discriminated Against Minorities, Women," *The New York Sun*, April 15, 2005, National section p. 7; Hansen, F., "Recruiting on the Right Side of the Law," *Workforce Management* Online, May 2006. Available online at: www.workforce.com/section/06/feature/24/38/12/. Accessed June 30, 2006.

[23] Stumpf, V., "Abercrombie & Fitch to Pay $40 Million in Settled Lawsuit," Californiaaggie.com, November 30, 2004, p. 1, available online at: www.californiaaggie.com/media/storage/paper981/news/2004/11/30/FrontPage/Abercrombie.Fitch.To.Pay.40.Million.In.Settled.Lawsuit-1318914.shtml?norewr ite200607191309&sourcedomain=www.californiaaggie.com. Accessed July 19, 2006.

[24] Greenhouse, S., "Abercrombie & Fitch Bias Case Is Settled," *The New York Times*, November 17, 2004, Section A, Column 4, National Desk p. 16.

[25] Gerstein, J., "Suit Charged Company Discriminated Against Minorities, Women," *The New York Sun*, April 15, 2005, National section p. 7.

[26] Hansen, F., "Recruiting on the Right Side of the Law," *Workforce Management* Online, May 2006. Available online at: www.workforce.com/section/06/feature/24/38/12/. Accessed June 30, 2006.

[27] "Clothier Settles Lawsuit Over Bias," *The Washington Times*, November 17, 2004, available online at: www.washtimes.com/national/20041116-115217-2037r.htm. Accessed December 23, 2008.

[28] See, "Executive Order 11246, As Amended," U.S. Department of Labor, available online at: www.dol.gov/esa/regs/statutes/ofccp/eo11246.htm. Accessed March 26, 2007.

[29] The U.S. Equal Employment Opportunity Commission, "Federal Laws Prohibiting Job Discrimination Questions and Answers," available online at: www.eeoc.gov/facts/qanda.html. Accessed March 21, 2007.

[30] Fisher & Phillips, LLP, "Meet the New ADA: Massive Changes Ahead for Nation's Employers," September 18, 2008. Available online at: www.laborlawyers.com/shownews.aspx?Meet-the-New-ADA:-Massive-Changes-Ahead-for-Nations-Emplo yers&Ref=list&Type=1122&Show=10879. Accessed January 14, 2009.

[31] Ibid.

[32] Office for Civil Rights, "Your Rights Under Section 504 of the Rehabilitation Act," U.S. Department of Health and Human Services, available online at: www.hhs.gov/ocr/504.html, Accessed December 23, 2008.

[33] U.S. Equal Employment Opportunity Commission, "The Age Discrimination in Employment Act of 1967," available online at: www.eeoc.gov/policy/adea.html. Accessed December 23, 2008.

[34] Georgetown University Law Center, "Laws Impacting Workplace Flexibility," Workplace Flexibility 2010, available online at: www.law.georgetown.edu/workplaceflexibility2010/law/adea.cfm. Accessed December 23, 2008.

[35] Resnick, Nirenberg, & Cash, P.C., 2009. "Age Discrimination," available online at: www.njemploymentlawfirm.com/PracticeAreas/Age-Discrimination.asp. Accessed February 17, 2009.

[36] The I-9 form is available online at: www.uscis.gov/files/form/I-9.pdf.

[37] Homeland Security, "E-Verify," December 5, 2008. Available online at: www.dhs.gov/xprevprot/programs/gc_1185221678150.shtm. Accessed January 14, 2009.

[38] "The Worker Adjustment and Retraining Notification Act," U.S. Department of Labor Employment and Training Administration Fact Sheet, available online at: www.doleta.gov/programs/factsht/warn.htm. Accessed December 28, 2008.

[39] See www.doleta.gov/programs/factsht/warn.htm.

[40] *Diaz v. Pan Am World Airways*, 442 F.2d 385 (5th Cir.1971).

[41] www.eeoc.gov.

[42] There are many free and fee-based sources of information on EEO and AA laws and regulations. The EEOC (www.eeoc.gov), OFCCP (www.dol.gov), and the Department of Labor (www.dol.gov) all offer compliance manuals and policy guidance online. Reference books that review and summarize permissible and impermissible practices as well as the outcomes of relevant court cases can also be useful. Fee-based information services including the Commerce Clearing House (CCH) and the Bureau of National Affairs (BNA) offer numerous employment law products and newsletters. Several professional associations including the Society for Human Resource Management (www.shrm.org) and the International Personnel Management Association (www.ipma-hr.org) also provide legal information to their members. Although some of the material is subscription-based, employment law web sites such as Ceridian Compliance Solutions (hrcompliance.ceridian.com) and the employment law practice center (www.law.com) also provide employment law news and resources.

[43] An excellent sample affirmative action program has been created by the EEOC and is available online at: www.dol.gov/esa/regs/compliance/ofccp/pdf/sampleaap.pdf.

[44] C. Andre, M. Velasquez, & T. Mazur, "Affirmative Action: Twenty-five Years of Controversy," Issues in Ethics, Summer 1992, 5(2), available online at: www.scu.edu/ethics/publications/iie/v5n2/affirmative.html. Accessed December 29, 2008.

[45] Labor Research Association, "The Growing Power of the Fortune 500," LRA Online, May 30, 2006, available online at: www.laborresearch.org/story2.php/417. Accessed March 26, 2007.

[46] Office of Federal Contract Compliance (2004). Affirmative Action Review: The Office of Federal Contract Compliance Programs (DOL). Available online at: clinton4.nara.gov/WH/EOP/OP/html/aa/aa06.html. Accessed January 3, 2009.

[47] E.g., *Steelworkers v. Weber*, 443 U.S. 193 (1979); *Wygant v. Jackson Board of Education*, 476 U.S. 267 (1986).

[48] Based on Breaugh, J.A., *Recruitment: Science and Practice*, 1992, Boston: PWS-Kent Publishing Company.

[49] *Wygant v. Jackson Board of Education*, 476 U.S. 267 (1986).

[50] *Regents v. Bakke*, 438 U.S. 265 (1978).

[51] *Grutter v. Bollinger*, 539 U.S. 306 (2003) and *Gratz v. Bollinger*, 539 U.S. 244 (2003).

[52] A. McBride, "Grutter v. Bollinger and Gratz v. Bollinger (2003)," The Supreme Court, December 2006, available online at: www.pbs.org/wnet/supremecourt/future/landmark_grutter.html. Accessed January 3, 2009.

[53] "U.S. Equal Employment Opportunity Commission: An Overview," U.S. Equal Employment Opportunity Commission, available online at: www.eeoc.gov/facts/overview.html. Accessed January 3, 2009.

[54] Hansen, F., "Recruiting on the Right Side of the Law," *Workforce Management* Online, May 2006. Available online at: www.workforce.com/section/06/feature/24/38/12/. Accessed January 3, 2009.

[55] Ibid.

[56] Greenhouse, S., "Abercrombie & Fitch Bias Case Is Settled," *The New York Times*, November 17, 2004, Section A, Column 4, National Desk p. 16.

[57] Hansen, F., May 2006.

[58] Equal Employment Opportunity Commission (2003). EEOC's Charge Processing Procedures. Available online at: www.eeoc.gov/charge/overview_charge_processing.html. Accessed January 3, 2009.

[59] The EEOC compliance manual can be found at www.eeoc.gov.

[60] The U.S. Equal Employment Opportunity Commission, Standard Form 100, Rev. 3-97, Employer Information Report EEO-1 100-118 Instruction Booklet, April 20, 2000, available online at: www.eeoc.gov/stats/jobpat/e1instruct.html. Accessed January 3, 2009. A sample EEO Standard Form 100 used for this reporting can be found online at www.eeoc.gov/stats/jobpat/eeo1.pdf.

[61] The OFCCP can be found online at www.dol.gov.

[62] U.S. Department of Labor (2004). All About the Employment Standards Administration. Available online at: www.dol.gov/esa/aboutesa/esaabot.htm. Accessed July 19, 2006.

[63] Hansen, F., "Avoid Getting Sued: Risks and Rewards in Recruitment Record Keeping," *Workforce Management* Online, February 2007, Available online at: www.workforce.com/section/06/feature/24/76/39/index.html. Accessed January 3, 2009.

[64] Office of Federal Contract Compliance (2004). Affirmative Action Review: The Office of Federal Contract Compliance Programs (DOL). Available online at: clinton4.nara.gov/WH/EOP/OP/html/aa/aa06.html. Accessed January 3, 2009.

[65] Quarles & Brady and Affiliates, LLP (2006). "Final OFCCP Rule Issued on Recordkeeping and Tracking of Race, Gender, and Ethnicity of 'Internet Applicants' ... An In-depth Analysis for Government Contractors," Employment Relations E-Mail Alert, November, available online at: www.edatab2b.com/monster/qb.pdf. Accessed January 3, 2009.

[66] *Federal Register* (2005). "Obligation To Solicit Race and Gender Data for Agency Enforcement Purposes." October 7, Volume 70, Number 194, pp. 58,945-58,963. Available online at: www.dol.gov/esa/regs/fedreg/final/2005020176.htm. Accessed January 4, 2009.

[67] Hoffman, V.J. & Davis, G.M., "OFCCP's 'Internet Applicant' Definition Requires Overhaul of Recruitment and Hiring Policies," *Legal Report*, January/February 2006, Society for Human Resource Management, 1-5.

[68] To narrow the pool of job seekers for which the contractor must solicit gender, race, and ethnicity data, contractors should identify as many basic qualifications as possible in their advertisements or, if not advertising, in their internal basic qualifications record, prior to considering any expressions of interest for that particular position. Although not specifically addressed in the rule, the OFCCP notes in the "Discussion of Comments and Revisions" preceding the rule that it encourages contractors to solicit such information through self-identification methods, such as electronic or traditional tear-off sheets.

[69] For additional information, visit the OFCCP's web site: www.dol.gov.

[70] Uniform Guidelines on Employee Selection Procedures, *Federal Register*, Vol. 43, No. 166, August 25, 1978. Available online at: www.dol.gov/dol/allcfr/ESA/Title_41/Part_60-3/toc.htm. Accessed January 4, 2009.

[71] Question and Answer No. 15, Adoption of Questions and Answers to Clarify and Provide a Common Interpretation of the UGESP, 44 FR 11998 (March 2, 1979).

[72] Frauenheim, E., "Internet Data Rule: Cloudy, But With a Silver Lining," *Workforce Management*, March 27, 2006, p. 46.

[73] Hansen, F., May 2006.

[74] This is known as a "McDonnell Douglas analysis"; See *McDonnell Douglas v. Green*, 411 U.S. 792, 802 (1973).

[75] Civil Rights Act of 1991. See usinfo.state.gov/usa/infousa/laws/majorlaw/civil91.htm.

[76] *Desert Palace, Inc. v. Costa*, 539 U.S. 90 (2003).

[77] *Griggs v. Duke Power Co.*, 401 U.S. 424 (1971).

[78] The Uniform Guidelines on Employee Selection Procedures are available online at: www.uniformguidelines.com/uniformguidelines.html. Accessed January 5, 2009.

[79] Uniform Guidelines on Employee Selection Procedures, Available online at: www.uniformguidelines.com/uniformguidelines.html, Section 4(D).

[80] See 42 U.S.C. § 2000e-2(k)(1)(A)(i).

[81] 42 U.S.C. § 2000e-2(k)(1)(A)(i).

[82] 42 U.S.C. § 2000e-2(k)(1)(A)(ii).

[83] Eiserloh, L.R., "Hiring, Firing, and Retaliation for Human Resources Personnel," 15th Annual Local Government Seminar: Employment Law Focus, April 10, 2002, Austin, Texas.

[84] Breaugh, J.A., 1992.

[85] Geyelin, M. & Green, W., "Companies Must Disclose Shaky Finances to Some Applicants," *Wall Street Journal*, April 20, 1990, B8.

[86] *Agosta v. Astor*, 120 Cal.App.4th 596 (July 12, 2004).

[87] Panus, V., "Make Sure the Picture You Paint Comes True," The Panus Report: Insights and Developments in the Law, Summer 2000. Reprinted in Small Business Monthly, July 21, 2006, available online at: www.kcsmallbiz.com/october-2000/people-power.html. Accessed January 5, 2009.

[88] Human Resource Advisor, "HR Policies and Practices: Hiring," Hr-esource.com, 2003. Available online at: www.hr-esource.com/index.asp?rightframe–hresources/sampleChapters/whrawSampleChapter_03.html. Accessed July 16, 2005.

[89] Panus, V., Summer 2000.

[90] CCH Inc., "What is Negligent Hiring?" Business Owner's Toolkit, 2004, available online at: www.toolkit.cch.com/text/P05_1510.asp. Accessed January 5, 2009.

[91] Steingold, F.S. & Bray, I.M. (2003). Legal Guide for Starting and Running a Small Business. Berkeley, CA: Nolo Press.

[92] "Employee Lawsuits: Negligent Hiring and Retention," USLaw.com, available online at: www.uslaw.com/library/article/carel5NegligentHiring.html?area_id=43. Accessed January 5, 2009.

[93] Barada, P.W., "What's Negligent Hiring?" Monster.com, 2004, available online at: hr.monster.com/print/?article=/articles/negligent/Index.asp. Accessed July 19, 2006.

[94] See "Did Hospitals 'See No Evil'?," CBS News, August 15, 2004, available online at: www.cbsnews.com/stories/2004/04/02/60minutes/main610047.shtml.Accessed March 22, 2007.

[95] Based on McCord, L.B., "Defamation vs. Negligent Referral," *The Graziadio Business Report*, Spring 1999, available online at: gbr.pepperdine.edu/992/referral.html. Accessed January 5, 2009.

[96] Ibid.

[97] Robert Kahn, "Violating a Noncompete Agreement Costs Ohio Firm Millions," *Workforce Management* Online, May 31, 2006, available online at: www.workforce.com/section/00/article/24/39/01.html. Accessed January 5, 2009.

[98] Thompson, E.C., "Secrets That You Keep," Security Products, January 2001, pp. 14-22.

[99] Kondon, C., "But It Was Just an Interview!" *Workforce Management*, January 2005, pp. 12-13

[100] The U.S. Equal Employment Opportunity Commission, "Federal Laws Prohibiting Job Discrimination Questions and Answers," available online at: www.eeoc.gov/facts/qanda.html. Accessed January 5, 2009.

[101] The U.S. Equal Employment Opportunity Commission, Best Practices of Private Sector Employers, 1997, available online at: www.eeoc.gov/abouteeoc/task_reports/practice.html. Accessed January 5, 2009.

[102] Ibid.

[103] Ibid.

[104] Ibid.

[105] The Federal Glass Ceiling Commission, "Good for Business: Making Full Use of the Nation's Human Capital," Fact-Finding Report of the Federal Glass Ceiling Commission, March 1995.

[106] Hansen, F., May 2006.

[107] The U.S. Equal Employment Opportunity Commission, 1997.

[108] The Federal Glass Ceiling Commission, "Good for Business: Making Full Use of the Nation's Human Capital," Fact-Finding Report of the Federal Glass Ceiling Commission, March 1995, pp. 28-29.

[109] Ibid, pp. 31-32.

[110] Hansen, F. "When Interviews Go Astray," *Workforce Management* Online, June 2006, available online at: www.workforce.com/archive/article/24/41/14.php?ht=hiring%20managers%20weak%20link%20hiring%20managers%20weak%20link. Accessed January 7, 2009.

[111] *Mathis v. Phillips Chevrolet Inc.*, 7th Cir., No. 00-1892 (10/15/01).

[112] The U.S. Equal Employment Opportunity Commission, 1997.

Index

legal defense 6
liability 6
"like me" bias 57, 58

M

major life activity 21
management lockout 9
Medicare 5
merit 1, 10, 27
military service 22
minorities 1, 26, 27, 32, 42, 58
    minority employees 28
    minority group 24
mixed-motive analysis 41
mixed-motive case 40
morale 7
motivating factor 40

N

National Labor Relations Act (NLRA) 6, 9, 10
national origin 22
native language 24
negligent hiring 48, 49, 50
negligent retention 50
negligent-referral claim 50
no cause 5
noncompete agreements 52
nondisclosure agreements 52
numerical goals 27

O

Office of Federal Contract Compliance Pro-
    grams (OFCCP) 31, 33, 34, 35, 36, 37
offshore companies 12, 13
Opportunity 2000 ... 33
organizational performance 2
outsourcing 12, 49
overqualified 58
overtime 12

P

part-time worker(s) 9
performance 50
    feedback 9
personnel policies 6
persons with disabilities 58
preferential treatment 27, 30
preferential-layoffs scheme 28
pregnancy 20
Pregnancy Discrimination Act 20
pre-hire agreements 10
prejudice 58
    prima-acie 34, 39, 40
reason 42, 45
privacy 49
    rights 49
promotion 26, 37, 39
promotion and transfer policies 9
proprietary information 52
protected characteristic(s) 23, 25, 40, 41
protected classes 26

protected group(s) 30, 41
punitive damages 32, 53

Q

quotas 25, 27, 29, 30

R

racism 58
random sampling 36
reasonable accommodation 21, 32, 61
recordkeeping 27
recruiters 58, 59
recruiting 39, 44
    recruiting and hiring practices 32
recruitment 3, 26, 29, 39, 46, 63
    effort(s) 23, 58
    practices 46, 61
recruits 46
references 51
Rehabilitation Act 21, 31
retaliation 6, 53
retaliatory discharge 7

S

safe workplaces 51
Sam's Club 17
screening process 46
seasonal worker(s) 9
selection rates 43
seniority 10, 28
    promotions 10
    provisions 9
sexism 58
sexual harassment 53
Social Security 5
Social Security Administration (SSA) 22
Social Security contributions 11
Social Security number 22
staffing 31
staffing practices 63
    statistical reports 40
    applicant-flow statistics 43
    concentration statistics 42, 44, 45
    flow statistics 42, 43, 44
    labor-force statistics 36
    statistical analysis 45
    statistical comparisons 45
    stock statistics 42, 43
stereotype 58
    characterizations 23
    stereotyping 59
strikes 9

T

Taft-Hartley Labor Act 10
talent 63
    pipeline 1
taxes
    employment 11
    incomes 5
    Internal Revenue Service 11

Acknowledgments

W e would like to thank our sons, Ryan and Tyler, for their support and patience while we wrote this book. We would also like to thank Pearson for allowing us to adapt some of the material from our book, *Strategic Staffing*, for use in this series. We also thank the reviewers — especially Laura Ostroff, director of Total Rewards and HRIS at Bon Secours Health System, Inc. — and the SHRM staff for this opportunity and for their suggestions and insights. If you have feedback about this book or if you would like to contact us for any reason, please e-mail us at phillipsgully@gmail.com.

About the Authors

Jean M. Phillips, Ph.D., is an associate professor of human resource management at the School of Management and Labor Relations, Rutgers University. Dr. Phillips is a current or former member of several editorial boards including *Personnel Psychology, Journal of Applied Psychology,* and *Journal of Management.* She received the 2004 Cummings Scholar Award from the Organizational Behavior Division of the Academy of Management and was among the top five percent of published authors in two of the top human resource management journals during the 1990s. She is also the co-author of the college textbooks *Managing Now!* (2007) and *Strategic Staffing* (2008) and consults in the areas of recruiting and staffing, linking employee surveys to organizational outcomes, and team effectiveness. She can be reached at phillipsgully@ gmail.com

Stanley M. Gully, Ph.D., is an associate professor of human resource management at the School of Management and Labor Relations, Rutgers University. He is a current or former member of the editorial boards of *Academy of Management Journal, Journal of Applied Psychology, Journal of Organizational Behavior,* and *Journal of Management.* He received multiple awards for his teaching, research, and service, including a research award from the American Society for Training & Development. His paper on general self-efficacy is in the top 10 most read papers in *Organizational Research Methods* and his meta-analysis on cohesion is in the top three most cited papers in Small Group Research. He is the co-author of *Strategic Staffing* (2008) and consults in the areas of recruiting and staffing, employee engagement, team effectiveness, and organizational learning interventions. He can be reached at phillipsgully@ gmail.com

Additional SHRM-Published Books

The Cultural Fit Factor: Creating an Employment Brand that Attracts, Retains, and Repels the Right Employees
By Lizz Pellet

The Employer's Immigration Compliance Desk Reference
By Gregory H. Siskind

Employment Termination Source Book
By Wendy Bliss and Gene Thornton

The Essential Guide to Workplace Investigations: How to Handle Employee Complaints & Problems
By Lisa Guerin

Hiring Source Book
By Catherine D. Fyock

Hiring Success: The Art and Science of Staffing Assessment and Employee Selection
By Steven Hunt

Human Resource Essentials: Your Guide to Starting and Running the HR Function
By Lin Grensing-Pophal

Leading With Your Heart: Diversity and Ganas for Inspired Inclusion
By Cari M. Dominguez and Jude A. Sotherlund

Outsourcing Human Resources Functions: How, Why, When, and When Not to Contract for HR Services, 2d ed.
By Mary F. Cook and Scott B. Gildner

Smart Policies for Workplace Technologies: Email, Blogs, Cell Phones and More
By Lisa Guerin

Stop Bullying at Work: Strategies and Tools for HR and Legal Professionals
By Teresa A. Daniel

Strategic Staffing: A Comprehensive System for Effective Workforce Planning, 2nd ed.
By Thomas P. Bechet

For these and other SHRM-published books, please visit
www.shrm.org/publications/books/pages/default.aspx.